The
THINGS That
MATTER
MOST

D0168093

Bob Welch

HARVEST HOUSE PUBLISHERS
Eugene, Oregon 97402

Cover by Left Coast Design, Portland, Oregon

Cover photo: Corbis Images

To Contact the Author

Write to:
409 Sunshine Acres Dr.
Eugene, OR 97401

or send e-mail to:
bwelch1@concentric.net

THE THINGS THAT MATTER MOST
Copyright © 2001 by Bob Welch
Published by Harvest House Publishers
Eugene, Oregon 97402

Library of Congress Cataloging-in-Publication Data
Welch, Bob, 1954–
    The things that matter most / Bob Welch
        p. cm.
    ISBN 0-7369-0376-3
    1. Life.   2. Values.   3. Christian life.   4. Baby boom generation—Conduct of life.
    I. Title.
BD431.W334   2001
248.4—dc21   20001016759

Printed in the United States of America

01   02   03   04   05   06   07   08   09   10   / BP-CF /   10   9   8   7   6   5   4   3   2   1

To Ann and Glenn Petersen,
who have chosen so wisely

ALSO BY BOB WELCH

A Father for All Seasons
Where Roots Grow Deep
Stories from the Game of Life

Contents

III. Purpose: Understanding Your Voyage ⌣ 85

IV. Strategy: Charting Your Course ⌣ 123

V. Courage: Raising Your Sails ⌣ 167

VI. Grace: Trusting the Wind ⌣ 197

Rigging the Boat

He stilled the storm to a whisper;
the waves of the sea were hushed.

They were glad when it grew calm,
and he guided them to their desired haven.

Psalm 107:29-30

TEN YEARS AGO, I BEGAN WRITING a book called *More to Life Than Having It All.* It was a book born of two polar-extreme experiences.

The first was working for a Seattle-area newspaper in one of the wealthiest communities in the United States: Bellevue, Washington. Microsoft founder Bill Gates, for example, built his $50 million lakeside home there; in fact, three of the country's seven wealthiest individuals now live within 15 minutes of where my family's $600-a-month rental stood. We joked that the fire hydrants in Bellevue spewed Evian, not plain old water. We played automotive poker at four-way stops, hoping for a royal flush—Mercedes, BMW, Rolls-Royce. We were among the few one-car families in our zip code area and certainly the only one with a '76 Rabbit that had moss growing from its rear floorboards.

The second experience, amid my brush with affluence, was visiting Mendenhall, Mississippi, among the poorest communities in the United States, and later spending two weeks in Haiti, the poorest country in the Western Hemisphere.

I still remember guarding the rear door of a makeshift medical clinic in Savane Carrée when a young mother lifted her child to me with pleading eyes that said: *Please, take my baby and make her better.* And I still remember returning home to America with the uneasy sense that, in a world that had so little, I had so very much—perhaps too much.

Ten Years of Perspective

Now, with a decade having passed and the world beginning a new millennium, my editors encouraged me to revisit the idea of materialism. Take the best of *More to Life,* they suggested, and blend it with stories you've encountered in the years since.

This book, about three-quarters of which is new, is the result. And given that our country, in the last ten years, has become only more firmly mired in the quicksand of consumerism, I believe it's all the more timely. We've never been more committed—if only subconsciously—to a material world.

We're in the midst of the greatest economic boom in U.S. history.

We want bigger houses. Since 1970, the average family size in the U.S. has *decreased* 16 percent while the size of the average newly constructed single-family house has *increased* 48 percent. And we buy those bigger houses because we work about a month longer per year, on average, than we did two decades ago.

Between 1995 and 1998 alone, about 1 million new millionaires were created. Baby boomers not only make up the richest generation of all time, but as their parents die, will benefit from the largest transfer of inherited wealth ever.

And yet accompanying our material riches has been an increasing sense of desperation, as if we're gulping down water and getting thirstier all the time. Because of the stock-market boom, 72 percent of Americans say they feel more pressure to buy bigger homes and swankier cars to keep up with their neighbors, reported *Newsweek* in 1999.

Equally disturbing: We're getting greedier. As affluence has increased, the percentage we give away has decreased markedly.

Since boomers began to come of age in the '60s, charitable giving as a percentage of our income has shriveled by 29 percent, according to Robert Putnam in *Bowling Alone.*

Ironically, as a new millennium dawns, we've become a people marked not only by prosperity, but by paradoxes. Since the 1950s, the average American's buying power has doubled, but surveys show that the number of those who say they're "very happy" declined from 35 percent to 30 percent.

By the year 2000, nearly a third of American children in grades eight through twelve owned stocks, bonds, or shares in mutual funds, the number having nearly doubled since just 1993—and yet, tonight, four in ten American children will go to sleep in a home in which their fathers do not live.

What's wrong with this picture? Materialism is in; relationships and true contentment are out, victims of our mad pursuit for fool's gold.

What Matters Most

Still, if I'm passionate about our reversing this life-in-the-fast-lane trend, I offer insight not as an infallible captain but as a fellow crew member who may know the ropes but sometimes forgets how to tie them.

"Only two sailors, in my experience, never ran aground," wrote Don Bamford in *Mainsail to the Wind.* "One never left port and the other was an atrocious liar."

I offer insight as someone who has seen both the haves and the have-nots, my 25 years as a journalist having offered up-close access to the lives of the rich and famous, and the poor and downtrodden.

I offer insight as someone who, in the last decade, has come to realize that life change happens more readily when we concentrate on what we *should* be, not on what we should *not* be.

Finally, I offer insight as someone who does not believe humankind has been shipwrecked on Planet Earth by some evolutionary storm, a mere accident whose future depends on a survival-of-the-fittest or figure-it-out-as-you-go mentality. Instead, any wisdom I offer is based on my belief that we were created by a loving God to live lives of deep purpose, a God who desires that none of us get "voted off the island."

One day, the book of Matthew tells us, Jesus was asked by a lawyer what the most important commandments were—in essence asked: What's the meaning of life?

"'Love the Lord your God with all your heart and with all your soul and with all your mind,'" Jesus said. "This is the first and greatest commandment. And the second is like it: 'Love your neighbor as yourself'" (Matthew 22:37-39).

Jesus did not say that what mattered was money, prestige, power, position, popularity, accomplishments, and a really good home entertainment center. Instead, He said what really mattered was *relationships*—with our Creator and with the people He created.

Yet many of us are caught in a cultural riptide that pulls us away from such treasures, toward the trivial. When we realize we're trapped in this undertow, we're faced with two choices: We can rationalize away the danger to avoid feeling guilty—or we can use our newfound awareness as an impetus to change—to return to the waters where we'll not only be safe, but where we'll thrive.

Each of the six parts of this book focuses on one of the ingredients of life change—awareness, vision, purpose, strategy, courage, and grace. Within each of these parts are stories of those same concepts at work in the lives of real people.

It's my hope that this book will at times make you laugh, at times make you cry, but above all will make you stop and think—as writing it has done for me.

When examining my own life, for example, I see this: someone who recently gave up a newspaper management position—plus $10,000 a year in salary, a hefty bonus, and a corner office—to take a columnist position that seemed a better fit for the gifts God has given me. But I also see someone whose life has become so burdened with busyness that sometimes it works against the very message of simplicity I espouse—someone who has changes to make himself.

Where We're Headed

The Things That Matter Most is less a how-to book than a why-we-must book, less nuts-and-bolts than heart-and-soul. And it's furled in a sailing theme, which seems to me appropriate for this voyage called life.

Much like life itself, sailing is soothingly simple and agonizingly complex. It is an adventure, a test of learning and growing and trying and trusting. And it can be flat-out exhilarating, which seems to fit the "abundant life" quest.

As I ply the waters of midlife, I sail a 22-foot Catalina—my mother's boat—at Fern Ridge Lake, not far from my house. There are two kinds of sailing: the lives-of-the-rich-and-famous variety, in which wealthy people stand Lands' End–like on boats roughly the length of a 747—and the Bob Welch variety, in which a middle-aged man happily casts off in a boat about the size of a minivan, then realizes his wooden rudder is slowly disintegrating and floating away, in pieces, in the wake.

"There is nothing—absolutely nothing—half so much worth doing as simply messing about in boats," Water Rat tells Mole in *The Wind in the Willows*. (I mainly mess about alone, my seamanship having sufficiently scared my occasional crew: wife Sally and sons Ryan, 21, and Jason, 18.)

I inherited my love of boats mainly from my father, who spent his life messing about in—and building—boats, sailboats in particular. As I write, I am flanked by a paintbrush permanently affixed in a chunk of well-dried fiberglass, a "trophy" accidentally molded in the bottom of a soup can by my father, a man whose boatbuilding forte was never cleanup.

My mother presented it to him as a way of chiding him for his forgetfulness.

I shared the whimsical trophy at my father's memorial service in 1996. My father was not a perfect man. And, like many of us, at times he focused too keenly on pursuits—boats, fishing, and photography were his passions—at the expense of people.

But he was a good man who let me build boats with him and who taught me to sail. And so when I look at that stuck-in-fiberglass paintbrush, I don't see my father's forgetfulness as much as I see my father.

I see a man who meant a lot to me—and still does.

I see a reminder to stop and laugh.

Above all, I see a relationship, which is what we're told our voyage should be all about.

At times, that voyage will be smooth and satisfying; at other times, rough and frightening, like a harrowing late-September morning I once spent sailing on Elk Lake, 5,000 feet up in Oregon's Cascade mountains, as a winterlike wind howled off the Three Sisters mountains. In either case, I believe our hope lies beyond circumstances, beyond the fickleness of an often-cold culture, beyond even ourselves.

If we are to find contentment beyond this have-it-all rat race, if we are to live lives of simplicity and meaning, if we are to invest in the stuff that really matters, our hope must lie within the God-breathed winds of grace. And in our willingness to alter our course—to come about—in order to let those winds take us where we need to go.

Thus does our voyage begin.

PART I

AWARENESS:

Watching Your Telltales

It is far better to not know where one is, and realize that one does not know, than to be certain one is in a place where one is not.

Lieutenant Barral, from *Digressions sur la Navigation du Cap Horn*, 1827

THE NEWSPAPER AD SHOWED photographs of two boats: One was an extravagant cruiser splashing boldly through a small wave. The other was a simple rowboat with two oars.

The cruiser, indicated the ad, was what you'd have if you did business with that financial service provider. The rowboat was what you'd have if you did not.

Though deceptively simple, the ad illustrates the materialistic equation that tugs at our hearts, minds—and souls—each day: the idea that bigger is better. The idea that something garish is better than something simple. The idea that something fast is better than something slow. And—no pun intended—the idea that if we do not choose big, garish, and fast, then we're somehow missing the boat.

At its root, the ad wants you to feel unhappy, discontent, lacking, inferior, temporary. Because materialism—in essence, the doctrine suggesting that *things*, not relationships, make the world go around—is a replacement for something else. And when we're content with that something else—the something else you can't buy with a credit card—we won't need to adorn our lives with the unnecessary goods and services being flashed before us at every turn.

We won't need to rumble wildly through life, trampling over self-perceived "enemies" and neglecting our once-significant families. We won't need to hang all our hopes on the rise of the stock market. We won't need awards and prestigious business titles and corner offices to make us pretend we "have it all" when, deep inside, where nobody is allowed to go, we know we don't.

Alas, at times as relentless as the sea—and, more often, as subtle as a glacial shift—our culture attempts to mold and shape us. (The average teenager will have seen 360,000 advertisements by the time he or she graduates from high school.) But sometimes we don't stop to notice what's going on around us because we're too busy following the leader, climbing the ladder, or playing king of the hill.

For example, does anyone actually believe we're more content because we now have hundreds of TV channels, rather than just a handful available to us? Frankly, I believe the increased options only magnify our discontent—we've become desperate channel surfers of life, trying to find something that will bring us the meaning that materialism will not.

But are we aware enough to notice? Marshall McLuhan, the late author and media expert, once asked: "If the temperature of the bath water rises one degree every ten minutes, how will the bather know when to scream?" Indeed, few of us slow down our frantic rush through life long enough to really assess where we are and where we're going—and how hot the water is getting. But most of us need to make some adjustments when it comes to what really matters: Essentially, we need to choose between the money and things that the world says are important and the relationships that God says are important.

Some of us may need only to tighten our sails and make better use of the wind. Some may need a complete course correction. And some may need to escape some relational doldrums that have left us emotionally and spiritually becalmed.

Looking Around Us

Regardless of where we're at, the first step in any quest for change is awareness: understanding ourselves, understanding our culture, and understanding our Creator.

To find out which way the wind is blowing, sailors watch cloth or yarn "telltales" hanging from the wire "shrouds" that anchor the mast in place. The best of the bunch develop a sensitivity to the wind by the touch of it on their face, forehead, or neck. Bottom line: They understand what's going on around them. And so must we.

"Be on your guard against all kinds of greed," says Jesus. "A man's life does not consist in the abundance of his possessions" (Luke 12:15).

In other words, be aware of the conditions around you, the cultural status quo that we can so easily accept—sometimes wholeheartedly embrace—even though it may work against our true purpose: the building of relationships.

It's important to be aware of the influences of culture because being aware of them helps us avoid becoming part of them. Not that the "more-more-more" mentality is anything new to America. By the early 1700s, Puritans in New England were espousing a faith in which wealth equaled spirituality. "The mercantile spirit flourished in Boston's busy streets, and its conformist preachers in the well-filled churches goaded on their complacent congregations to amass yet more wealth as an outward symbol of inward grace," writes Paul Johnson in *A History of the American People.* "Thus America's success was undermining its divine mission: 'There is danger lest the *enchantments* of this world make them forget their *errand into the wilderness.*'"

Nearly three centuries later, the enchantments of this world persist, though never extolled with more coast-to-coast fanfare than during the rise of yuppiedom in the 1980s. Said *Newsweek* magazine: "What Yuppies have discovered is nothing less than a new plane of consciousness, a state of Transcendental Acquisition, in which the perfection of their possessions enables them to rise above the messy turmoil of their emotional lives."

Now, many such people have morphed into what author David Brooks calls "Bobos"—baby boomers who have blended the bourgeois '80s with the bohemian '60s, a grand way to give their go-mad materialism a hip image as they ease their BMWs down life's homestretch.

Being Aware Changes Us

Alas, as convenient as it is to neatly label a certain group as materialistic—*them*—we do so, in part, to take the focus off ourselves—*us.* Too often, we think of materialism as something *out there.* But it's really *in here.* In our hearts. It doesn't begin with us making a purchase; it begins far deeper, with who we are, how we see the world, how we see our place in that world, and ultimately, how we see God.

Do we, for example, see ourselves as deprived because we perceive we have less than others?

Gaining awareness changes how we think and act. Many of us, largely because of the advertisements that incessantly remind us of it, come to believe that we're pathetic little rowboats in a cabin-cruiser world. Here's the real perspective: If the entire world population consisted of a mere one hundred people, one would own a computer and one would have a college education. Eighty would live in substandard housing, seventy would be unable to read, fifty would suffer from malnutrition. Six would possess 59 percent of the world's wealth, and all six would be citizens of the United States.

But in America, we are constantly reminded of how painfully hard we have it. Who can forget the credit-card commercial with the couple in the airport, having just returned from vacation. "We were almost there," the woman says wistfully, as if to suggest that with a little more vacation time they could have broken free of the gravity of real life. Now, they have arrived back at Reality International and life is once again empty.

Suddenly, they get an idea: Why not just pull out the credit card and take off on another trip? Bingo, they're off, buying clothes, laughing, eating exotic food. The moral of the commercial? That you can get to the elusive Land of Fulfillment—you can really *get there*—with a plastic card. And, more subtly, that we're deprived; one vacation at a time is not enough.

The past decade has only pulled us more in that direction. Television incessantly pounds the Land of Fulfillment into our heads—and the average U.S. home has its television on 7 hours and 11 minutes a day, up 32 minutes from 1992, when *More to Life* hit the bookstores.

Ten years ago, the Internet was in its infancy. Now marketers have a whole new way of tempting us with their wares; we call up our messages and are flooded with come-ons for "can't-miss" moneymaking opportunities, from offshore investments to 2.9-percent credit cards.

Awareness helps us stave off such come-ons.

Awareness lets us face our pasts and understand that the value we place on *things* and *relationships* has been influenced by the value our *parents* placed on things and relationships. The idea isn't that we're *unalterably* slaves to our pasts—but that we are if we don't *face* those pasts, as happens when the Ghost of Christmas Past rattles Scrooge until he faces his past.

Awareness gives us perspective, opens our eyes, opens our minds—to not only the bad stuff but the good stuff. One of the funniest—and most profound—cartoons I've ever seen shows a couple walking down the beach, the woman wearing headphones, the man having just taken his off. "Wow," says the guy, "when you take off your headphones you can hear the roar of the surf!"

When you gain awareness, when you broaden your perspective, when you stop and consider that if you own a house you are already wealthier than 95 percent of the people on the planet, you'll understand that you're blessed.

Where Are We?

While in Mississippi, I was talking to a young boy in one of the poorest counties in America. He showed me his house, which was old and tattered and small. Then he asked me to describe my house. At the time, I lived in what most Americans would consider a middle-class rental. No garage. A basement remodeled into living space. Carpet that was 20 years old.

"Man," he said, with wonder in his voice, "you live in a *mansion*."

I had never, for an instant, thought of myself as living in a mansion; truth be known, there were times when, living in one of the richest communities in America, I considered myself deprived. But the young boy gave me some much-needed perspective.

Where, indeed, do we live? Where are our hearts? In short, where *are* we? Good sailors know that before they can reach their destination, before they can leave the moorage, before they can even plot a course, they must know where they are. They must get their bearings. And the best way to do that is to have a fixed point—a lighthouse, a buoy, a point of land, *something*.

For some people, that fixed point—what they set their sights on—is the Joneses next door or the slinky women on the magazine covers or popular opinion or tarot cards or a TV evangelist or intuition or tea leaves or science or education or fads or some seminar leader who promises peace and prosperity for a mere $499 (workbook and tapes not included). For some people, it's self. And for some, it's nothing at all; they choose instead to go with the cultural flow—a poor choice given the current of greed and violence that dominates the six o'clock news.

My fixed point, in a metaphoric sense, is the stars—"A compass can go wrong," says a Tongan adage, "the stars, never." My fixed point, in a literal sense, is the Maker of those stars, the Maker of the seas on which we sail, the Maker of us all: God.

In Psalm 8:3, the psalmist celebrates this relationship of God, place, and people in words:

> *When I consider your heavens,*
> *   the works of your fingers,*
> *the moon and the stars,*
> *   which you have set in place,*
> *what is man that you are mindful of him,*
> *   the son of man that you care for him?*

These words evoke a universal theater, in which we—people—have been placed at center stage. But no unfeeling director has given us lines and said, "There now, *read these.*" Instead, we've been given the freedom to say what we want. To do what we want. To chart our own courses.

Like life itself, sailing affords a keen sense of freedom, a sense of freedom that can be deceptive. For example, as elegant as a sailboat may appear when gliding on a downward reach—wind blowing from its stern—it is in constant danger of something called an *unexpected jibe.* When that happens, the wind catches the wrong side of the boom and slaps it across the boat with gusto, cracking anything in its way, including heads.

If wind shifts can cause unexpected jibes, so too can sailors who aren't paying attention to what's going on around them. "The danger in jibing, as in most things, results not from deliberation but inadvertence, not from caution but heedlessness," writes Richard Bode in *First You Have to Row a Little Boat*.

In our quest to live simple, purposeful lives, we need to know which way the cultural winds are blowing, lest we be victims of an unexpected jibe, or gradually veer off course.

What We've Lost

In the ten years since *More to Life* came out, we've drifted, McLuhan-esque, farther from the relationship-based life God wants us to live and closer to a materialism-based life that God wants us to avoid.

We see the subtle signs of it—does anybody buy a used car anymore?—and the more conspicuous signs of it: Even in the Northwest, where people have traditionally worn their wealth in subtle earth tones, exclusive communities, some with million-dollar homes, are springing up. Faxes and cell phones and palm-top computers—though offering certain practical advantages—have, for some, become high-tech slavemasters. Despite an almost unprecedented lining of American pockets, charitable giving has plummeted: in 1960, we gave away about one dollar for every two we spent on recreation; in 1997, we gave away less than 50 cents for every two dollars we spent on recreation, according to *Bowling Alone*.

The actual *things*—the houses and cars, the trivial pursuits and toys—are not the problem; they're just *symptoms* of the problem. The real problem is *what we give up* to have the things. It's the compromises we make when we let a job or toy or recreational pursuit become our priority, be those compromises in time with our children, in attention we give our spouse, or in something else.

Since 1993, the proportion of youths who own stocks, bonds, or shares in mutual funds has more than doubled, reaching 31 percent. But survey after survey shows, although adults may be investing more *money* in their children, they're investing decidedly less *time* in those children.

Our pastor once gave us a two-part quiz. On the first part, he asked us to list the five wealthiest people in the world, the last five Heisman Trophy winners, and the last five winners of the Oscar for Best Actress. Few of us were able to remember any of these people.

Then he asked us to write down the names of a few teachers who had helped us through school, five people who have taught us something worthwhile, and a few people who have made us feel appreciated and special. It was easy.

The point? The people who make a difference in our lives are not the ones with the most credentials, the most money, or the most awards. They are the ones who cared. They are the people with whom we've built *relationships.*

As a culture, we need to get our bearings. And realize that we're far better off admitting we're adrift than pretending otherwise. It's only when we admit we're lost that we have any hope of being found. Only when we seek that have any hope of finding. Only when we check our telltales that we see which way the wind is blowing.

Less Can Be More

I think of those two boats in the magazine ad. The big, fancy cruiser, at first glance, seems to promise so much. Yet I see how easily you could get so caught up in the gadgetry that you'd forget about anyone else aboard. I see how, having a computerized control panel, you'd feel little satisfaction in getting yourself from Point A to Point B by your own skills. And how, high up off the water, you'd miss so much along the water's edge.

Meanwhile, the little rowboat, at first glance, seems to promise so little. Yet I see, as with sailing, the value in having to row the boat to get somewhere—the same satisfaction you feel when backpacking to some high-mountain lake. I see the value in processes, not just results; in the means, not just the end.

I see how, with a small, simple boat like that, you could hear the water slapping the hull and could nudge the reeds at lake's edge. You could not only marvel at geese flying in formation high above you, but see them up close, after their splashdown for the night.

Being so closely attuned to all that was around you—the graceful glide of those geese on the water, or the person sitting in the seat across from you—you might never even hear the mad rush of commuter cars on the road nearby.

Where I Belong

With the freeway ahead of us and home behind, the photographer and I left on a three-day newspaper assignment. We were bound for the Columbia Gorge, where the Columbia River carves a mile-wide swath between Washington and Oregon; where windsurfers come from across the country to dance across waves created by "nuclear winds," where I would be far from the world of nine-to-five and deadlines and routines and errands and rushing kids to baseball practice.

Far from the "R-word"—responsibility.

Frankly, it had not been the perfect farewell. Our family was running on empty. Our aging car was showing signs of automotive Alzheimer's. We were all tired, cranky, and trying to shake colds.

My then eight-year-old son tried to perk us up with an off-key version of a song from the musical *Annie*, reassuring us that the sun *would* come up tomorrow.

It didn't work. I had been busy trying to get ready for the trip; Sally had been busy fretting because my three days of freedom were going to mean three days of added responsibility for her.

"Daddy, are you coming to hear my class sing Thursday night?" Jason, our eight-year-old, asked amid the chaos of departure.

Had I been Bill Cosby, I would have gotten a funny expression on my face, said "Well, of course," and everyone would have lived happily ever after. But I didn't feel much like Bill Cosby that morning. "I'm going to be out of town," I said. "Sorry."

Giving Sally a quick kiss, I was on my way. Now, hours later, I was far away from family, free from the clutter, the runny noses, the demands on my time.

Knowing little about each other, the photographer and I shared a bit about ourselves as we drove. Roughly my age—I was in my mid-30s at the time—he was married but had no children. He and his wife had seen too many situations where couples with children had found themselves strapped down, scurrying for babysitters, and forced to give up spontaneous trips.

He told me how he and his wife had recently taken a trip to the Gorge by themselves. My mind did a double take. *By themselves? What was that like?* Long ago, in a universe far, far away, I vaguely remembered what it was like: taking off when the mood hit. No pleas for horseback rides about the time you're ready to crash for the night. No tornado-swept rooms. No meet-the-teachers nights.

Besides having no children, the photographer had no six-month-old french fries on the floor of his car, no legs of Superman action figures on his dashboard, and no road maps on which most of Washington had been obliterated by a melted Snickers bar.

Where had I gone wrong?

For the next couple of days, despite the threat of rain, we explored the Gorge for a feature section—thousand-foot walls of basalt rising on either side of the Columbia River, fluorescent-clad sailboarders, like neon gnats, carving wakes in the water.

If the land and water were intriguing, so were the windsurfers. There were thousands of them, nearly all of them baby boomers, spending their days on the water, their nights on the town, their mornings in bed.

About every fourth car had a board on top. License plates from all over the country dotted the streets. Some of these "board heads" were follow-the-wind free spirits who lived out of the back of vans; others were well-established yuppies who were here for a weekend or a vacation.

In the evenings, the hub town on the river turned into Oregon's version of a California beach town: boomers eating, drinking, and being merry, lost in frivolity and freedom.

For me, seeing this group was like discovering a lost, ancient tribe. You mean, while I was busy trying to fix jammed bike chains, these people were jamming to the rock beat of dance clubs? While I was depositing paychecks to be spent on groceries and orthodontics bills and college funds, these people were deciding what color sailboards to buy?

Where had I gone wrong?

On our last night, the cloudy weather continued, which irked the photographer and mirrored the mood that had overcome me; we both needed sunshine, only for different reasons.

As I stared from the motel room at the river below, I felt a sort of emptiness, as if I didn't belong. Not here. Not home. Not anywhere. Just as the winds of the Gorge were whipping the river into whitecaps, so were the winds of freedom buffeting my beliefs.

Marriage. Children. Work. I had anchored my life on such things, and yet now found myself slipping from that fixed position. Had I made a mistake? Had I sold out to the rigors of responsibility? Someday, when I was older, would I suddenly face the bitter reality of regret, wishing I had gone with the wind like the others?

I was getting ready for bed when I spotted it—a card in my suitcase, buried beneath some clothes. It was from Sally. The card featured cows—my wife is big on bovines—and simply said, *I'll love you till the cows come home.*

I stared at the card for a number of minutes. I repeated the words in my mind. I looked at the same handwriting that I'd seen on love letters in college, on a marriage certificate, on two birth certificates, on a will.

As I went to bed, there was no need to call the front desk and ask for a wake-up call. I'd already gotten one. The card bored through my hardened heart, convicted my selfish conscience, refocused my blurry perspective. I knew exactly where I needed to be. Exactly where I belonged.

The next day, after a two-hour interview, six-hour drive, and three-block sprint, I arrived at my son's school, anxious and out of breath. The singing program had started 20 minutes before; had I missed Jason's song?

I rushed into the cafeteria. It was jammed. Almost frantically, I weaved my way through a crowd of parents clogging the entrance, to where I could finally get a glimpse of the kids on stage.

That's when I heard them: 25 first-grade voices trying desperately to hit notes that were five years away from being hittable. *The sun would come out tomorrow...*

My eyes searched this collage of kids, looking for Jason. Finally, I spotted him: front row, as usual, squashed between a couple of girls whose germs, judging from the look on his face, were crawling over him like ants at a picnic. He was singing, all right, but with less enthusiasm than when cleaning his room.

Suddenly, his eyes shifted my way and his face lit up with the kind of smile a father only gets to see during a grade-school singing program when his child's eyes meet his. He had seen me, a moment that has stayed frozen in my memory for more than a decade.

Later, through a sea of faces, I caught sight of Sally and my other son. After the program, amid a mass of parent-child humanity, the four of us rendezvoused, nearly oblivious to the commotion around us. I felt no emptiness, only connectedness.

How could one man be so blessed?

In the days to come, I resumed my role in life as bike-fixer and breadwinner, husband and father, roles that would cause a windsurfer to yawn. *But for all the excitement of riding the wind,* I decided, *I'll take the front-row smile of my eight-year-old son.*

And for all the freedom of life in the Gorge, I'll take the responsibility of loving the woman who vowed to love me till the cows come home.

Of Saints and Poets

IN A SMALL TOWN ON THE southern Oregon coast, I once gave the keynote speech at a writers' conference. I had made the repeat visit for a number of reasons, not the least of which was a Saturday afternoon fish fry that featured a small band called the Sophisto-Kats, two guys in their 60s and 70s on the organ and drum, who played such songs as "Pennsylvania 6-5000" and "Has Anybody Seen My Gal?"—and did so with such an understated sense of "cool" that I mentally smiled my way through the entire lunch.

If Hollywood were filming a movie that had a scene from a small town on the Oregon Coast, it would cast the Sophisto-Kats, who wore matching vests and caps accented with musical notes. During mid-song when someone dropped a buck in their tip jar, they smiled and nodded.

The young poets who had read their works after my talk the previous night were not at all like the Sophisto-Kats. The poets were mainly baby boomers. Brooding baby boomers. Brooding baby boomers who wore jeans and sandals. One woman wore a beret.

Most of the poetry they read was gloomier than winter on the Oregon coast, and a few poems not only pushed the boundaries of good taste but went flying over the edge. These poets had such an overstated sense of cool that, at times, I mentally cringed.

But thinking about the Sophisto-Kats and the Brooding Poets reminded me that each brought something good to the table of life: The musicians brought the unbridled joy of innocence and celebration of simplicity. They played songs that uplifted the human spirit, that reminded us of love, that paid tribute to a simpler time when people mattered.

But the poets dared to go deeper. Though they didn't show many signs of figuring it out, they at least fiddled with the Rubick's cube of life. They questioned. They wondered. They probed.

If the Sophisto-Kats offered only the "sunny side of the street," the poets read of the seamier side of the street.

Both are laudable, considering that life is made of each, that Scripture deals with each, that Ecclesiastes reminds us that "to everything there is a season, and a time to every purpose under the heaven."

One poet touched me deeply with his piece on an abusive childhood. One woman wrestled with the loss of her mother, unlocking in the process some wrestling of my own with the loss of my father.

What poets do best, I believe, is notice the world around them. We may not always agree with what they conclude about what they find, but at least they *look*. At least they touch, taste, smell, and feel. At least they don't spend their lives mindlessly staring at the blue glow of a television set, without bothering to explore, think, wonder, or question the life they've chosen.

For all their brooding, at least they live, as Thoreau called it, the "examined life." At least they lead *deliberate* lives, carefully considering, like the sculptor, whatever it is they're making of themselves.

We live in a world that's loathe to look at itself in the mirror. Why? Because of what we might see, of course. If we race through life, if we immerse ourselves in enough *stuff*— some of it significant, some not—we can rationalize away our avoidance of the mirror. What we seek, though we may not even notice it, is diversion.

Writes Blaise Pascal, the French mathematician and religious philosopher:

What people want is not the easy peaceful life that allows us to think of our unhappy condition, nor the dangers of war, nor the burdens of office, but the agitation that takes our mind off it and diverts us. That is why we prefer the hunt to the capture.

That is why men are so fond of hustle and bustle; that is why prison is such a fearful punishment; that is why the pleasures of solitude are so incomprehensible.

We have become, essentially, a culture that immerses itself in the trivial and ignores the significant. We can, with the touch of a few keystrokes, access on the web a cache of information far greater than humankind has ever known. But too many of us seem afraid to look at ourselves, our God, and the culture around us. We can name the final four on TV's *Survivor* series, but can't name four of the Ten Commandments. We can carry on deep, intellectual conversations about government greed, but don't dare explore the "charitable giving" column of our financial spreadsheets.

Writes Pascal: "Man's sensitivity to little things and insensitivity to the greatest things are marks of strange disorder."

In Thornton Wilder's *Our Town,* Emily, who has died while giving birth to her second child, is given a chance to witness the day she turned 12. In doing so, she realizes all the nuances of life she had never seen.

"It goes so fast. We don't have time to look at one another. Goodbye world….Goodbye to clocks ticking…and Mama's sunflowers. And food and coffee. And new-ironed dresses and hot baths…and sleeping and waking up. Oh, earth, you're too wonderful for anybody to realize you…Do any human beings ever realize life while they live it—every, every minute?"

"No," replies the stage manager, then pauses. "The saints and poets, maybe—they do some."

Emily, it seems, is part Sophisto-Kat, part poet. She appreciates the innocent goodness of ticking clocks and hot baths and yet, like the poet, ascribes a deeper meaning to it all. She not only looks at the embroidery from the back side, where the patterns, with no context, offer only a disheveled road map to nowhere, but turns it over and sees that all these seemingly insignificant zigs and zags ultimately comprise something. It's called life.

Frankly, too many of us don't live life; we let life happen to us. We sleepwalk through it. We live only the life of the Sophisto-Kat, so lost in the innocence of the past that we miss the wonder of right now—and the deeper stuff that lives beyond the keyboard. Or so afraid of facing ourselves should the music end that we don't dare stop playing.

If not the Sophisto-Kat, we live the life of the poet, so lost in examination and doubt that we miss the sunny side of the street. So tied to our persona as Life Cynic that we don't dare emerge from the brooding shadows, though we secretly want to. But we stay put, stay safely where we've always been, fastened firmly to an image that has become something of an idol.

Somewhere between brooding poet and carefree musician lies a special place where we can benefit from a touch of each. We would be wise, I think, to find it.

Big Life

"GO, BABY, GO, BABY, GO!"

"C'mon, faster, faster, get goin'!"

The shouts of my two sons, then six and three, were coming from the patio as I worked at home, many years ago. What I needed was quiet. What I got instead was children cheering. But cheering what?

"What's going on out there?" I asked, mildly miffed at the noisy intrusion.

"Nothin', Dad," said my six-year-old. "We're just racin' caterpillars. Wanna race one?"

I politely declined, explaining that I had *important stuff* to do. But in the years since then, I've learned a simple, but profound, truth: Racin' caterpillars is important stuff, too. Real important stuff.

Awareness, I've realized, sometimes comes in a size Small. As parents, sometimes we need to be willing to get down on our hands and knees and experience life—look closely at life— from our children's perspectives.

That's not easy, I know. We are—*ahem*—adults. We are involved in what my youngest son, when he was small, called "Big Life." We pay taxes, tie Windsors, speak four-syllable words, fight traffic, attend seminars. Then, suddenly, some freckle-faced six-year-old in a Nike sweatshirt is asking us to *puh-leeze* play freeze tag with him.

So we do what any self-respecting parent would do. We squirm out of it somehow. *Too tired. How 'bout if I just stick in a video for you?* Or *How about tomorrow, sport?*

It has almost become a cliché to urge parents to spend more time with their children. But what I've learned as a parent is that we need to spend more than just time. We need to spend "kid time." Especially when our children are young.

Instead of reading a book on a park bench while little Amy swings, we need to be swinging next to her. Instead of listening to a game of hide-and-seek from inside the house, we occasionally need to hide and seek. Instead of jogging the track while the kids play soccer, we need to be the goalie.

In short, we need to spend time *with* them, not just *around* them. To participate, not observe. To create our own fun, together, rather than buying it at some arcade. And, yes, to get a little wild and crazy, even if it means being the only parent in the neighborhood who sleds when it snows or gives his kid two bags of marshmallows at his birthday party and lets the critters have an all-out marshmallow war.

The idea isn't to forego our responsibilities as parents—teaching and disciplining our children, praying for them, and modeling a good husband-wife relationship for them. The idea is to supplement such things by stepping into our children's world—not to stay permanently, but just to visit from time to time.

Ecclesiastes 3:1 says there is an appointed time for everything. I like to think there's a time for serious talks, worship, and study. And a time for piggyback rides, knee football, and sleeping out back on a summer night, listening to crickets.

Remember how good you felt as a child when—and if— Mom and Dad showed up for your third-grade open house at school? It was because they were stepping into your world, a day-to-day world where they seldom ventured. Somehow that gesture made you feel important, gave you a certain worth. For one evening every term, your parents would look closely at your stick-figure drawings and feeble attempts at cursive. They'd sit at your desk in one of those miniature chairs—not just anybody's chair, but the very chair you sat in every day— and look at life at your level.

Too often, as our children are growing up, we get caught up in the Madison Avenue–inspired act of turning them into Instant Adults. But what my now-nearly-grown children taught me, especially in their younger years, is that children desperately need childhoods.

One summer, my boys set up a Kool-Aid stand. Seeing they had made only 60 cents by noon, I realized two things: First, I'd made a major marketing mistake by choosing to live on a cul-de-sac with no drive-by traffic. Second, while I considered their venture a failure, they considered it a complete success. To me, 60 cents meant disappointment; to them, it meant pure gold—or at least a pack or two of baseball cards.

Adults are results-oriented; children are process-oriented. To me, the Kool-Aid stand was only a wagon, a scrawled sign, and two pitchers of slightly red water. To my sons, however, it was an adventure.

Adults go fishing to catch fish; children go fishing for the *experience* of catching fish, to see how a worm squiggles, to wonder where fish sleep at night, to watch a leaf swirl in an eddy.

Adults want the perfect experience; children just want fun—and tend to find it even when we don't. One drizzly day at the coast, Sally and I sat in a restaurant, lamenting the absence of the blue skies we'd eagerly anticipated for our vacation. Across the table, the boys didn't have time to be down; they were too busy having fun by breaking soda crackers into the shapes of U.S. states.

"What's this, Dad?"

"California?"

"Naw, California's way bigger. Idaho."

"Sure—of course. Idaho."

Going from Big Life to Small Life sometimes creates difficulty. Balancing the roles of Authority Figure and Human Horse can lead to problems if your children don't understand what mode you're in at a given moment. Besides that, it can be hazardous to your taste buds; those of you who have eaten a peanut-butter-and-ketchup sandwich know what I mean.

But it's worthwhile making ventures into the Candylands of our children's lives. Each trip, though it may seem insignificant at the time, helps build a bond between parent and child that will last long after the game has been put away or the sled has been stored in the attic or the Kool-Aid stand has returned to simply being a wagon again.

Because now that they're older, our boys don't remember the stuff Sally and I bought them or the videos we rented them, but they can tell you nearly every detail about the fort we built them out of wood pallets, including the day we dedicated it with an official flag-raising.

To them, this was Big Life—and, for us as adults, it should be Big Life, too.

Some 15 years have passed since that day, and the video of that event is somewhere in our library of memories. But more importantly, it is locked forever in the minds of two once-small boys who will remember it as not just a dedication of a fort, but a validation of their worth.

Everybody Welcome

I DON'T OFTEN FEEL LONELY. But on a drizzly Sunday night in December 1999 I found myself all alone in a town along Lake Ontario, Canada, three time zones from home. I was in the midst of a book-publicity tour and had nothing to do. And I felt lonely. I didn't belong. I missed my family.

Actually, I like being alone more than most people, I think. But this wasn't one of those times. I had been gone for a couple of days and had seen thousands of people in airports and hotels and on freeways, but there's nothing like being a stranger amid throngs to remind you you're alone. It's like being the only kid at the pool without an inner tube.

All of which is to say that the sign appealed to me when I saw it in front of the church: It said a "Candlelight Festival of Nine Lessons and Carols" was going to be held that very night. And at the bottom it said, in bold letters: "Everybody Welcome."

To me, a guy who goes to a nondenominational church that frowns on candles because they ruin the carpet during weddings, that sounded pretty cool.

Naw, I'd just be the kid without the inner tube.

But this is a church, I countered in my mental game of ping-pong. God's people! And the sign said "Everybody Welcome." And if God says our priorities are to be relationships, then shouldn't these folks be interested in a relationship with me?

After all, I'm part of *everybody*.

But they don't really mean it; it's just a traditional greeting, like when we say to someone, "How are you?" We don't really want to know. We don't expect someone to actually tell us, particularly if they aren't "fine," which is what we want and expect everyone to say, right?

On the other hand, the church wouldn't bother to say that if it didn't really mean it, would it?

But the people won't make me feel welcome, I rationalize. They'll act like I don't belong.

But I'm a lonely guy, far from home, in search of some Christmas cheer.

But that's overstating it. I sound too desperate. Only desperate people show up at churches on a whim—like in *Home Alone*, when the little boy thinks the burglars are after him and has nowhere else to go.

I should go to the service.

But their ways may not be my ways. If we sing, they may sing different songs than I want to sing. They could get wrapped up in all that highfalutin *liturgy*—that's a scary word for a recovering Episcopalian—and what I think might be a warm and celebratory evening might turn out to be a lifeless going-through-the-motions evening.

Another thing: The whole service might be in English *and* French, which could mean a really long night. Just about everything in this part of Canada is done in English and French; the phone book has the Customer Guide page of contents and the *Guide du Client;* not only how to make Emergency Calls, but how to make *Appels d'Urgence.* I half expect to order a burger and find half of it to be meat, cheese, and ketchup, and the other half cordon bleu.

Let's face it, I'm not a desperate enough man to show up at this service. Someone else needs the Festival of Carols more than me, someone running from burglars. All I'm running from is loneliness.

But if we don't risk, if we don't at some point say, if even in the subtlest of ways, *I'm needy,* how can anyone meet our needs?

But I'm not needy enough. The kids in Kosovo—they're needy. They need warmth and shelter and the smile of someone who cares. I have a wife and a family and friends and a home church and a credit card that can give me instant cash. What needs have I?

Yeah, but for two days I've been walking around airports and hotels. I've watched college kids step off planes and into the arms of tearful parents. I've watched people strolling along Lake Ontario, arm in arm. I watched some plumbing company hold its Christmas party in the lakeside restaurant last night while I ate alone.

Where is the Lonely Guy Needs Assessor, the woman behind the desk in the bifocals who looks at your application and decides whether you qualify?

But if I don't qualify, will someone take the spot in the church I would have had? Will someone take the seat I would have sat in and enjoy the Nine Lessons and Carols that I did not? And if that someone doesn't show, then will I feel worse, sitting alone in a hotel room and watching a game of curling, a sport that—no offense to Canadians—seems like part shuffle-board, part sweeping the kitchen?

That's it. I'll go to the service.

No, it will be a bust. The name of the service sounds neat but the service will be a drag. As usual, I'll expect too much and be disappointed. If I don't go, then no way will I be disappointed.

There. Done. This time for sure. It's getting darker. All is calm, all is bright. The clouds, like the weather woman said, are rolling in, and the geese—would they call those America geese since we call the ones down south Canada geese?—are landing on the lake. They look cold, but you wonder: Are they really? You just assume that God found a way to keep them warm.

But what about us? Not the geese in the lake, but the people surrounding the lake? Those around us assume we're warm but sometimes we're not. Sometimes we look like we're all together, but emotionally, we need to make an *Appels d'Urgence.*

So this, I come to realize, is a little bit like being lonely all the time. This is what it's like to be the Non-Churched. These are the mind games you play before deciding to take a risk and see if you'll step out of the darkness and into the light, and be welcome.

Final decision: I go. I step into the church. It is beautiful. Not ornate, but woodsy traditional with symmetry and candles and stained glass.

It has everything. Everything but what I need: Someone to welcome me. Not with some sort of red carpet. But just someone to make contact. Or shake my hand. Or say "Merry Christmas." Just someone to notice I'm there.

But much as I like stories with happy endings, it doesn't happen. The choir starts singing songs, and I think that this will lift my spirits. But the choir sings as if it's not really sure that this kid in the manger was really God come to Earth. Midway through the Nine Lessons—about the top of the fourth—I want to scream: *Rejoice! For unto you is born this day in the city of David a Savior, which is Christ the Lord!*

Children come to the front of the church to sing. They are beautiful: black, white, Indian—and radiate joy. But when they're finished singing, just as I'm ready to begin feverish applause, I realize this is a no-applause church.

The choir drones on. I at least find meaning in the words, if not in the lack of spirit with which they're sung.

Finally, in the bottom of the seventh, I slip out the back door—nobody seems to miss me—and walk back to the hotel, still alone.

What if I truly had been a full-time lonely person—not just a part-time lonely person—looking for the light? I feel ashamed being part of a faith that talks the talk of reaching out but sometimes doesn't walk the walk.

Then I think one of those thoughts you wish you hadn't thought: about how often a service at our church ends and I'm quick to hobnob with friends rather than seek the face of a stranger. How I'm quick to remember some "really important" task I need to do so I can rationalize that I can't go meet someone new; after all, I have Important Church Stuff to attend to.

A light rain starts to fall as I approach the hotel where my warm room awaits. The geese on Lake Ontario are quiet. A lone man slumps next to a building.

Where do they all belong?

Front Porch

I WAS IN BRITISH COLUMBIA RECENTLY, when I noticed something odd about the houses. At first, I couldn't figure out what it was. Then it dawned on me: They had front porches.

Remember front porches?

They're like soda shops, one of those good things that faded away without most of us noticing. Older neighborhoods—and a few new houses here and there—still have them. In other regions of the country, particularly the South, front porches still dominate. But where I live, front porches—large, bona fide, sit-in-a-rocking chair porches—are rare these days.

And that says something about life in America at the turn of the millennium. Our grandparents and parents grew up in a world full of porches. At the end of a summer day, the folks sat on the porch and watched the world go by.

It was a place to catch up on who was doing what in the neighborhood. A place to think. A place to read the evening paper, to talk, to sip lemonade, and to listen to distant dogs barking and pint-sized baseball players arguing close calls at home plate.

In other words, a place where you were aware of the world around you.

Pop, a farmer and my wife's grandfather, would make special chairs out of old tractor seats so he and Gram could sit on the porch.

In the '50s, suburbia arrived. Traffic increased. A friend of mine fortunate to have a wonderful front porch says he and his wife never sit on it anymore. "Too noisy," he says.

More than anything else, today's lack of front porches is metaphorical, a symbol of an inward-oriented culture that contradicts Scripture's call to be outward-oriented people. "Do nothing out of selfish ambition or vain conceit," writes Paul in Philippians 2:3-4, "but in humility consider others better than yourselves. Each of you should look not only to your own interests, but also to the interests of others."

Even the interests of the folks who live around us.

In the last four decades, we've become a more private society. With the advent of air conditioning, many people needn't go outside to stay cool on a summer night. When we do, we've retreated to the back yard, building patios and decks and hot tubs and gazebos. We've built fences to separate us from neighbors—more here in the Northwest, I've noticed, than in the South and Midwest. We've even developed members-only neighborhoods with gates and guards and magnetic cards.

A friend who recently moved into a new suburban neighborhood noticed how seldom he sees his neighbors. In the morning, the automatic garage-door openers click and people leave for work; in the evening, the automatic garage-doors click and people come home from work. But nobody is ever *seen.* Our homes have become hermetically sealed from the rest of the world—airtight architectural Baggies in which nothing touches us.

A sociology professor was telling me how, amid such cultural shifts, teenagers are caught in a sort of no-man's-land. Once, a teenager was accountable not only to his parents, but to a lesser extent, his neighbors. Now, his parents are too busy for him, and he doesn't even know his neighbors, much less feel any sense of obligation to—or support from—them.

Television, videos, and computers—not the peace of the front porch—have become our post-dinner magnet. Once, a couple might have spent an evening talking or watching the sky bid good night. Now, too many of us spend our summer evenings sitting in front of entertainment centers, being pulled away from each other by whatever's on the tube instead of toward each other by what might be on our minds or hearts.

In a sense, porches are everything our modern times are not. These are high-tech times; porches are low-tech places. These are fast-paced times; porches require time. These are action-oriented times; porches don't do a thing.

Porches accompanied more innocent times, when young lovers held hands on them, and when George and Mary embraced in *It's a Wonderful Life* and the T-shirted neighbor yelled from his own front porch, "Why don't you kiss her 'stead of talking her to death?"

And yet, what porches represent—a place to be still and examine ourselves and the world around us—seems to be a need that abides, despite the differences in the decades.

In a world where it's easy to get wrapped up in technology, in the nonstop drive to have it all, something has gotten lost. Something important. Cell phones are ringing and beepers are beeping and people are dashing from here to there, some in cars with computerized navigational systems.

But we could still benefit from having a place where we can talk, a place to think, a place to read, smell a summer breeze, sip lemonade, and listen to distant dogs barking and pint-sized players arguing close calls at home plate.

Safely Ashore

AT AGE 41, HE HAD WRAPPED PROSPERITY around him as if it were a down comforter guaranteed to stave off the biting wind of anything that might blow his way.

Like a twentieth-century Horatio Alger, the Seattle man I'd come to know had risen from a small-town, middle-class background to acquire big-city clout. His income as a financial consultant exceeded $200,000 a year, and he was in demand as a seminar speaker. He and his wife lived in a nice home in the safe environs of suburbia. They vacationed in Europe and cruised the Caribbean.

None of which mattered to the man now. Alone in his den on a rainy February afternoon, he wept uncontrollably. Forgotten were all the evenings he had spent punching the numbers on the calculator, making sure he and his wife's nest egg was secure. Forgotten were all the days at the office, boldly beating back the competition to fortify his financial fortress.

All along, he had been expecting the enemy to come from somewhere else—a flat market, an underestimated competitor, a jealous employee. Instead, the enemy had attacked from within.

He was in the throes of a nervous breakdown. And, he figured, there was only one way out.

☾   ☾   ☾

IN HIS PARENTS' EYES, THIS WOULD BE the ultimate disgrace: a grown man crying. He had been raised to believe that, regardless of your vulnerabilities, you "never let 'em see you sweat." Appearance was everything. His mother masked her inferiority complex by dressing in perfect outfits and keeping an immaculate lawn and garden. His father masked his insecurities by attaching his identity to work and little else.

He was raised in that ever-so-cozy-sounding-but-not-always-so-warm environment of the "Christian home." But this was not a family whose values went deep in the spiritual soil; it was a family that, in essence, was rooted deep in the things of the material world.

After he was involved in a sledding accident as a boy, he got so much special treatment from his parents that he became spoiled. He found it hard to make friends. And he made himself a promise: *I'll show them. When I grow up I'm going to make more money, and be more successful, than all of them.*

He worked his way through college. Afterward, he sold insurance and ultimately got into financial consulting.

He got married, but it was a stormy relationship from the start. Like his parents, he lived a dual life. He preached Christian principles but lived his own.

He didn't want any children; he was too selfish, he says. Instead, he amassed more and more money. He regularly stretched his work day to 10 and 12 hours. He became irritable and insensitive to others, particularly to his wife. She called him "King Tut."

His life's motivation was simple—and deceptively dangerous: fear. Fear that he would lose his business. Fear that he would lose his prestige. Fear that he would lose his identity as someone who had made it in the world.

But, remembering a cue from his past, he never let 'em see him sweat. He bought only tailor-made suits for the same reason his mother wore only the finest dresses. He bragged of his accomplishments. His list of clients became more and more prestigious. People became tools, things he could manipulate to get what he wanted.

Though he wasn't averse to spending money, he wasn't addicted to it either. Spending money wasn't his security; *having* it was. He would go home in the evenings, sit in his den and crunch the numbers, making sure his protection was there. He would analyze the situations and plan the moves needed to fortify his stronghold.

The more money he made, the more invulnerable he felt and the less he believed he needed anyone else, particularly God.

Work, accumulate, analyze, plan. That was the rhythm of his life, a pattern that continued for years and years, until he found himself getting depressed more often and more easily. He began dreading going to work. He couldn't sleep. He was on the brink of divorce.

Work, accumulate, analyze, plan. The strategy wasn't working. Finally, on that afternoon in the den, the man crumbled from the inside out.

The nervous breakdown lasted for months, though he continued to work. He would find himself crying uncontrollably, rolling on the floor, mentally tortured by his own thoughts.

Then—the idea, the faint flicker of a way out: End it all. One squeeze of the trigger. Why not? What good had he brought anyone? Who would miss him?

The regret about his selfishness ate at him like acid. Once, his wife came home from work and found him in the middle of the street, yelling at the top of his lungs, "God, forgive me!…God, forgive me!"

He would later describe his breakdown as something nobody could understand unless he had been through it. Compared to a nervous breakdown, he said, "depression is a trip to Disneyland."

He describes it as sitting in a boat in the middle of a lake, knowing you're unable to swim. There are no life jackets aboard and suddenly the boat springs a leak. The water starts rising, first to your ankles, then to your knees, then to your neck. Finally, you sink—only to find that you're in just four feet of water.

But he did not reach for a gun. After the torment came the determination to change. For all its pain, the breakdown had forced the man to examine his life for what it really was, not for what he pretended it to be.

What he saw wasn't pretty—a selfish, insecure man who professed to be a follower of Christ but refused to give Him control.

A Christian counselor helped him understand himself, why he had become who he was and how he could change. He immersed himself in Scripture, particularly the Psalms.

> *Save me, O God,*
> *for the waters have come up to my neck.*
> *I sink in the miry depths,*
> *where there is no foothold.*
> *I have come into the deep waters;*
> *the floods engulf me.*
> *—Psalm 69:1-2*

He realized that God has promised to forgive our selfishness. And he prayed fervently. The result was something akin to a summer rain that breaks a 12-week drought. He realized that it wasn't important what he accomplished. What was important was who he was—and how that played out in the lives of the people around him.

He reconciled with his wife, asked for, and received, her forgiveness. He cut back his time at work considerably. People who knew him said he was more willing to show his vulnerabilities instead of hiding them behind a tailored suit, more willing to admit a mistake than blame someone else. More sincere. More empathetic. And no longer using people as pawns.

There's a difference, he realized, between happiness and joy. Happiness is self-centered and depends on circumstances; joy is others-centered and rises above circumstances. Happiness is superficial; joy is deep.

In a world that promises all sorts of quick-fix solutions to the challenges we face as human beings, the man found that what triggered his turnaround—in essence, what saved his life—was humility: his willingness to finally look at himself for what he'd become.

Only then, with God's grace, was he able to get safely ashore from the middle of the lake.

PART II

VISION:

Seeing Your Destination

There is no pleasure sailors have greater than sighting from the deep the distant land.

Plautus

WHEN I WAS 16, I EMBARKED ON WHAT I considered a fairly adventurous trip: sailing an eight-foot pram from our campsite at the west end of Oregon's Cultus Lake to the Snodgrass family's campsite, about 500 feet away.

When Robin Graham was 16, he embarked on a fairly adventurous trip of his own: sailing a 24-foot sloop, *Dove,* on what would become a 33,000-mile, five-year trip around the world.

OK, so the magnitudes of our adventures were slightly different. That explains why I was thrilled to have the chance to interview Graham years later, after I'd become a features writer for a Seattle-area newspaper and Graham had retreated to the wilds of Montana to build a log house, raise a family, and live off the land.

How could you not be intrigued by someone who had thumbed his nose at the status quo and circled the globe at an age when most of us were just trying to get the nerve up to ask someone to the prom?

"My own tyrants were peanut butter sandwiches and people in gloomy offices who insisted I wear shoes, people determined to arrange my life in tidy patterns, prodding me this way and that until I could be safely sent out into society, wearing white collars and gray suits, credit cards in my billfold, golf clubs in the closet under the stairs and a half-paid-for car in the garage," wrote Graham in *Dove*.

So he began dreaming of something else. Began dreaming of fulfilling his passion to sail the high seas, alone. "I loved the smell of rope and resin, even of diesel oil," he wrote. "I loved the sound of water slapping hulls, the whip of halyards against tall masts. These were the scents and sounds of liberty and life."

Thus did Graham ease out of San Pedro Harbor in Long Beach, California, on July 27, 1965, to conquer the world.

Bigger, Better

Though you can argue about the practicality of such a voyage—I can't imagine giving a 16-year-old son of mine a thumbs-up for such an adventure—you have to admire this about Robin Graham: He not only had the awareness of where he was; he had a vision for where he needed to go.

How many people today live moored to regret because instead of setting sail for some higher purpose, they've anchored themselves to the false security of affluence?

How many people have bought into Graham's credit-cards-in-the-billfold nightmare simply because they knew of nothing else?

How many people dare to dream—not the shallow dreams of wealth and fame and making a name, but the deeper dreams, rooted in connecting with those people around them?

If the first step in living a more meaningful life is *awareness*—getting our bearings about where we are—the second is *vision*: realizing where we need to get to. The first is akin to *looking* at ourselves in the mirror; the second to *imagining* how we might need to change.

Though at the time, Robin Graham didn't fully understand his motives, he looked at life and saw a pointlessness to it all, and imagined how he could change that.

What Graham found was the Great American Irony: Less is often more. In essence, he chose not the extravagant cruiser featured in that newspaper ad, but the tiny rowboat—and found that the marketers had it all wrong: Bigger *wasn't* better.

"At sea, I learned how little a person needs, not how much," he wrote after his journey.

It is the same concept that programs such as Outward Bound use in helping at-risk youth get in touch with themselves and with life: Spend two weeks in the wilderness and you not only may find out how little you need to survive, but you may learn to live apart from the addictions you thought you couldn't live without.

And really, what distinguishes many people from others these days is only the difference in their addictions. Is the 50-year-old woman who compensates for her unhappiness with four-figure mall binges any different from the anorexic young woman or the drug-addicted young man? Each, in a sense, is trying desperately to fill an emptiness with something that will never satisfy.

For Robin Graham, choosing "bigger and fancier" was to rob himself of the chance to build calluses of character from rowing the boat himself—or, in this case, manning sails and handling a tiller himself.

In fact, what made his journey so fulfilling was that he chose a small boat to take on a big ocean. What made the experience fulfilling, you see, wasn't the *result*—not the idea that, after five years of sailing, he could proudly slap a bumper sticker on the back of his car that said I SAILED THE WORLD—but *the journey*. Not the inevitable fame that came upon his final docking in 1970, but the immeasurable satisfaction of knowing he'd fulfilled his vision with five years of blood, sweat, and tears.

Wealthy but Disappointed

In *The Writing Life*, author Annie Dillard tells of an aspiring young photographer who, each year, would bring his best work to an honored photographer for judgment. Each year the old man looked at the prints and separated them into two piles. Each year the old man placed a particular landscape scene in the bad stack. Finally, he had to say something.

"You submit this same landscape every year, and every year I put it on the bad stack. Why do you like it so much?"

"Because," the young photographer said, "I had to climb a mountain to get it."

If the American Dream seems to no longer satisfy those who long for it, perhaps it's because we no longer have to climb a mountain to reach it. The soaring stock market and get-rich-quick dot-coms have rolled enormous wealth into millions of bank accounts in the last decade, but we seem to be a people still hollow and hungry.

"The main emotion of the adult American who has had all the advantages of wealth, education, and culture is disappointment," writes author John Cheever.

Oh, but we mask it so well. Rationalization is a powerful thing; it temporarily soothes the soul while simultaneously skewing our vision. In a *Self* magazine article, Michael Korda extols the virtues of being money-happy. "I'm profoundly skeptical about the value of postponing pleasure, nor do I believe that depriving yourself of something you want is necessarily good for the soul," he writes. "On the contrary, good for the soul is self-gratification, in my view."

What Mr. Korda conveniently fails to acknowledge is that such choices ask a price. Self-gratification, for example, might well mean a man leaving his family to have an affair; though Korda and Hollywood might consider this a semi-heroic "following one's heart," I doubt it would be seen this way by the wife and children left behind. Self-gratification is always a glorious romp—though fleeting—for the self-gratified; it is something quite different for those abandoned in the quest.

It is easy to put words together to defend our life choices; what's harder is waking in the middle of the night, feeling the gnaw of emptiness that we never share with anyone else.

I think of a man I once wrote about, whose home was worth well over $1 million and whose swanky cruiser bobbed lazily at his backyard dock. But one day, he shot himself to death. For me, his death was one of those "all-that-glitters" messages, a reminder of the vulnerability of those who appear to have it all together but do not.

Wrapping ourselves in wealth to protect us against the cold is as old as man. In America it flourished, in particular during the Enlightenment, or Age of Reason, when influential thinkers such as John Locke, Thomas Jefferson, and Benjamin Franklin punctuated the idea that life was built on a foundation of the scientific, the material, and the secular, not the spiritual. And nearly two centuries later, other than a small back-to-simplicity movement that marked the 1990s, this notion shows few signs of abating.

In fact, a soaring stock market and plethora of upstart Internet companies during those same '90s infused materialism with new energy. In the yuppified '80s, villains were made of the suddenly wealthy; the icon of greed was Gordon Gekko (Michael Douglas), the slimy protagonist in the movie *Wall Street*. Since then, however, the wealthy have been given a sort of Good Housekeeping Seal of Approval. Never mind that, as former Labor secretary Robert Reich says, "It's the first time in the postwar era that so many people seem to be getting so rich with so little relative effort on their part."

Our Relationship to Our Possessions

Outwardly, Americans appear utterly content. We are the stuff of TV minivan commercials, all children and dogs and newness. Alas, my years in journalism have shown me that many who appear so secure in their wealth are, in the words of Thoreau, living "lives of quiet desperation."

Why? Because though we can wrap ourselves in the American Dream, it cannot protect us from our own worst enemy: ourselves.

There's nothing inherently wrong with owning a nice car or landing a prestigious job or having a corner office; materialism rears its ugly head only when such things become, in essence, our priorities. Our idols. The place we put our hope. The replacement for something that's missing.

Likewise, vision-skewing materialism is not reserved for the wealthy; in fact, it's an equal-opportunity force, subtly sabotaging not only the rich but all who yield to its powerful pull.

It has less to do with how much we have than with how much the things we have *mean* to us. I have been in an expensive lakeside home whose owner seemed much more concerned about arranging an expensive surgery for a young Haitian girl burned in a fire than about making the cover of *House Beautiful*, though his house would easily qualify. Likewise, I have been in a welfare apartment with a tenant who spent her days watching an extravagant big-screen TV setup and smoking dope—while neglecting her two children.

Who is the more materialistic of the two?

It's far easier, of course, to evaluate the lives of others than to evaluate our own; as I've written this book, I've been humbled by the realization that I need to make some course changes myself. It begins, I realize, with slowing down.

Seeing Things Clearly

When we slow down, we see more clearly. And without such vision, the voyage is doomed—as says Proverbs 29:18: "Where there is no vision, the people perish: but he that keepeth the law, happy is he" (KJV).

In many ways, America has lost its vision. Once land of the free and home of the brave, we've become enslaved by the insidious clutches of consumerism; we've become the home of the quick fix, regardless of the price.

Consider divorce, once seen as a traumatic fracturing of humankind's most significant relationship: marriage. In the past three decades, we've gone from the point where couples would ride out the worst storms to preserve their marriages to the point where couples part over conflict so minor that our grandparents would have scoffed.

Don't repair your marriage, we say; throw it away. Don't change; flee. Don't accept the reality that every marriage has irreconcilable differences; run.

Despite the cultural currents, I see hope. The general media is finally acknowledging what Christian writers have said for decades: Children don't handle divorce as if it were nothing more than a rearranging of the living room furniture. It hurts, often for a lifetime.

Sometimes, vision may bark an all-hands-on-deck command: We've wandered dangerously close to the shoals and need drastic measures to stay safe. Other times, vision may whisper assurance: Stay the course, but hold steady on that tiller.

After reading a magazine article of mine, a woman wrote a letter to me that I found inspiring—because she was holding steady on that tiller, despite it not being easy.

> I'm a happy woman. I am married and have three little kids. I used to go out with some friends—four or five women, most of them single—and we would talk a lot about our lives.

Because of this, sometimes I would wonder if I had chosen the right life, with kids, a husband, a house to care for. My single friends seemed to have a better life. They could travel more than me, they had more time for fun, they could spend all their money on themselves. But then, sometimes they would tell me that they wanted to have my life, with a husband to share experiences with. A calm life. I agreed, but I was not sure which life was better.

One day I was going back home after one such meeting, and I was thinking about my life and theirs. As soon as I arrived home, one of my kids saw me and gave me a wonderful smile and a big hug. Then I understood. This is where I belong. My kids and my husband are more important for me than anything else. I am blessed.

Our culture too often paints the family- and faith-oriented life as a miss-the-boat life, a mundane life, a restricting life. But that's only the case if we ignore the richness found in relationships.

A close friend of mine often talks of life being either a nightmare or an adventure. It depends, he says, on whether we dare to dream—dare to envision a higher purpose than the tired pattern of accumulating and spending, accumulating and spending, accumulating and spending...dare to trust in something beyond what we can see.

When we fix our dreams to the one heavenly Star, we aren't guaranteed smooth passage wherever we sail. But we are guaranteed a voyage of substance, not superficiality.

The Irish folk hymn "Be Thou My Vision" says it well. Therefore do I anchor for the night with these words:

Riches I heed not, nor man's empty praise,
Thou mine inheritance, now and always:
Thou and Thou only, first in my heart,
High King of heaven, my Treasure Thou art.

High King of heaven, my victory won,
May I reach heav'n's joys, O bright heav'n's Son!
Heart of my own heart, whatever befall,
Still be my Vision, O Ruler of all.

A Wild Call

STAYING OVERNIGHT ON A 22-FOOT SAILBOAT with your two
boys is like trying to change your clothes, cook, and go to the
bathroom in a floating phone booth—only without being able
to call 9-1-1 if you, say, realize you're suffering from scurvy.

Ah, but I was younger then, and John Masefield's poem
"Sea Fever" tugged at the bow lines of my soul.

> I must go down to the seas again, to the lonely sea
>   and the sky,
> And all I ask is a tall ship and a star to steer her by...

The words were ingrained in me almost subliminally, all
because of my father: For a few years, he worked for the state
system of higher education making educational films, one of
which had something to do with the 1902 poem by Masefield,
Great Britain's poet laureate.

He hired Harry Sackett, a local high school drama teacher,
to dress up as a sea captain. He built a model sailing ship and a
miniature wave tank, complete with a sky painted on the background. (Did other people's fathers do this kind of stuff?)

Then each evening, for what seemed like weeks, my father
filmed the ship gallantly plying the food coloring–dyed waters
of the wave tank—and the drama teacher reading Masefield's
poem with great flair.

> And the wheel's kick and the wind's song and the
>   white sail's shaking,
> And a gray mist on the sea's face and a gray dawn
>   breaking...

The finished product looked remarkably like a high school drama teacher wearing a fake beard, and a plastic model ship bobbing in a makeshift wave tank. It had all the realism of one of those 1950s sci-fi movies in which the giant crabs looked amazingly like regular-size crabs made to look large.

But if the realism wasn't particularly memorable, the poem was. Night after night, it was the last thing I heard before drifting off to sleep.

> *I must go down to the seas again, for the call of the*
> *running tide*
> *Is a wild call and a clear call that may not be denied;*
> *And all I ask is a windy day with the white clouds*
> *flying,*
> *And the flung spray and the blown spume, and the*
> *sea-gulls crying.*

Thus I've come to believe it was this subliminal message, and not reason, that prompted me to suddenly suggest that I take the boys for an overnighter on board my parents' Catalina sailboat. Why else would an otherwise semi-sane man volunteer for such an adventure?

My wife, Sally, loved the idea. Of course she would; she wasn't going. Being the odd woman out meant a quiet night at home, meant being able to lounge around in a 2,000-square-foot house instead of being wedged in with three other people in a cabin that's roughly 6 feet wide, 11 feet long, and 4 feet from top to bottom.

That's 66 square feet or, to make the accommodations sound a bit more reasonable, 264 cubic feet. Using cubic feet actually is more appropriate than square feet, in that it sounds as if you're spending the night in a refrigerator, which, give or take a few feet and degrees, is an apt description. If you subtract 20 cubic feet for our three bodies, each of us was left with about 80 cubic feet in the cabin.

The great challenge of having three people on a boat that size is, whenever you want to put something away or get something that's been put away, you or someone else is sitting on it or leaning against it. And so getting something or putting something away is a little like trying to paint a ping-pong table while on top of it—and with a game in progress: very difficult business.

Nevertheless, in the summer of 1992, we set sail one Friday night for the marine version of sleeping out back. After an uneventful voyage, we anchored in the far reaches of Fern Ridge Lake. I dropped anchor, tied it off, turned to the boys, and said, "Well, we're here."

"Now what?" said Ryan, at 13, the ever-enthusiastic rear admiral of this boat.

"Yeah," said Jason, at 10, Ryan's equally enthusiastic seaman recruit, "now what?"

With the family-pleasing demeanor of the *Wonder Years* mother, I said, "Well, dinner, of course."

"Yippee," muttered one of the crew members.

Not to be deterred by this underwhelming expression of enthusiasm, I went into the cabin to fix dinner, which consisted of unwrapping a handful of precooked hot dogs from aluminum foil. We crammed them into our mouths, added a few chips for flair, and called it good.

"Now what?" asked the crew, not much for simply immersing themselves in the *experience.*

My mental telltales fluttered lightly with the idea I might have a mutiny on my hands. But over the years, I'd learned something: Children are far more resilient and imaginative than we think. They would, I figured, find things to do. I needed to cut them some slack; if they didn't soon engage this adventure, I would simply maintain my captainly composure and, well, have them walk the plank.

I peeled off my shirt, took off my sandals, and jumped overboard. Soon the boys joined me for a sunset swim.

Sometimes kids simply need an adult to prime the pump. Sometimes kids have the most fun when they realize *you're* having fun.

I started the theme song from *Jaws* and lurked behind them like a shark.

"Are there fish in this lake?" Jason asked.

"There are carp in this lake," I said. "But they grow as big as sharks. In fact, some people say they're more danger—"

"Aaaaaaaaaaaaaaaaaaaaaaaaaaaaaaaaaah!"

The boys took turns jumping from the boat and climbing up the back ladder. I pulled out my camera and started taking pictures. Soon the sun slid behind the Coast Range and the sky was making that zillion-pixeled shift from blue to pink, courtesy of late-August smoke from nearby grass-seed fields that farmers had burned off after harvest.

In the cabin, Ryan adjusted the radio's dial, looking for a broadcast of the local minor-league baseball team, the Eugene Emeralds. At the stern, Jason coaxed California gulls with leftover hot dog buns.

I read two pages of a book. Then I looked up, lost in the moment—the shift from day to night, the flutter of a gull's wings, the muted cadence of a baseball announcer—*3-2 pitch, swung on, strike three!*—and realized I had slipped into one of those Perfect Moments.

That's when it happened. Fear gripped me with an intensity that only a sailor far from shore can know: I had to go to the bathroom, an urge straight from Masefield's poem—

> *…a wild call and a clear call that may not be denied…*

Our boat had, in sailing terms, a "head." But you must understand: This was not The Love Boat. With three people constantly bumping into each other, sometimes it was not even

The Like Boat. This was not even a boat with a cabin that you could stand up in. Remember? Four feet from top to bottom.

Going to the bathroom in the cabin of a 22-foot sailboat is a prayerful experience, for a couple of reasons. First, with such a small boat rocking back and forth, courtesy of boat wakes, you almost need divine guidance to hit the target. And second, because of the low ceiling, you must go on bended knee. But I did it, and emerged from the 24-cubic-foot bathroom with a subtle sense of accomplishment and a desire to never have to do that again as long as I live.

Ryan scrounged around in the cooler.

"Another Pepsi, Dad?"

"Uh, no," I said. "Definitely not."

Darkness descended. We pulled out the Monopoly board and, with the metal car, hat, and thimble doing admirable jobs of not sliding with the sway, engaged in a raucous game. We bought, sold, visited jail, went to jail for good, paid a school tax of $150, and celebrated winning second place in a beauty contest. We laughed. Argued. And boasted. Eventually, my journal recalls, Jason won, having successfully thwarted my goal of securing the lucrative North Carolina, Pacific, and Pennsylvania Avenue stretch.

We snacked: Licorice. Gummy worms. Pop. Hardy food for hardy sailors.

We told a few stories.

We unrolled our sleeping bags. The boat's brochure said, "The interior offers comfortable sleeping accommodations for a family of four or five." This was a slight overstatement, like those "Robert S. Welch, you have won $100 million" letters, or those billboard advertisements that show giant burgers that never quite look like that when you unwrap them at the fast-food restaurant—instead, they look like burgers that have been left on the seat of a bus for a few days.

The boys slept in a bed that was converted by lowering, as the brochure referred to it, the "dining room" table. I slept outside, under the stars, on a fiberglass shelf that was about three-and-a-half inches longer than my body and two-thirds as wide. Down below, the boys squirmed, jabbed, and made a few of those bodily noises that nobody wants to hear anywhere, much less in a 264-cubic-foot space.

They laughed and joked and fought, and when encouraged by the captain to go to sleep, quickly blamed one another for not being able to do so. Their talking turned to whispering and finally to blessed silence. Both were asleep.

All was quiet, save for a few party frogs in the nearby reeds. The lake was completely still, giving a finality to the day that you seldom sense on land. All was dark except for the stars above and the faint glow of light from the city to the west.

Somewhere out there in that glow of light sleeps my wife, I thought. *Down below, like hellions-turned-angels, sleep my beautiful sons. And here I lie, looking up at the night sky.*

> *He wraps himself in light as with a garment;*
> *he stretches out the heavens like a tent*
> *and lays the beams of his upper chambers on their*
> *waters.*
> —*Psalm 104:2-3*

Vision—the ability to imagine where you need to get—is a word of grandeur. It connotes vast, sweeping horizons; grand plans; big adventures requiring much time and planning. And yet vision sometimes is grand in a simple way. Sometimes vision is nothing more than seize-the-moment spontaneity.

In the summer of 1992, our one-night trip seemed so very small. And yet it gets larger all the time. I see two photos upstairs in our home: both of little boys caught in mid-air at one five-hundredth of a second, crystal clear, jumping from the decks of *At Last,* into the waters of Fern Ridge. Both have arms and legs outstretched. Both have wild smiles on their faces, smiles that remind me how important it is to follow the stirrings of your soul when the sea beckons.

> *I must go down to the seas again, to the vagrant*
> *   gypsy life,*
> *To the gull's way and the whale's way, where the*
> *   wind's like a whetted knife;*
> *And all I ask is a merry yarn from a laughing fellow-*
> *   rover,*
> *And quiet sleep and a sweet dream when the long*
> *   trick's over.*

The Healing

AT 70, HE PONDERS HOW HE'S DIFFERENT because he was once there, in Korea, fighting a war that some have called nothing more than a "police action." A Marine, Jim McKee remembers it as something a bit more intense, considering he recently awoke from a combat nightmare and rammed his fist through the bedroom wall.

"Well, for one thing," McKee says, then stops, the words suddenly stuck. He pauses, regroups. "For one thing, I've never been able to hug my children."

His four children, two sons and two daughters, are in their 40s now. "The doctors say I don't want to get too close to people because, like in war, I fear they'll be dead tomorrow."

For the past year, McKee has been part of an uncommon therapy group: six to eight veterans of World War II and Korea confronting the demons of war, some for the first time. Men in their 60s and 70s. Men more commonly linked with John Wayne than Alan Alda. Men who are still wounded, though their wars are long over.

If relationships are to be our priority, it's important to recognize that we each face obstacles in trying to start, maintain, and mend those relationships. War, particularly the painful memories of war, can be such an obstacle.

I have great respect for all who have fought in wars; I have all the more respect for those who years—sometimes even decades—later have the vision to seek help to become better husbands, fathers, and friends.

When discharged, vets were expected to pick up their lives where they left off. In an irony he sees only now, 74-year-old

Monty Hershberger returned from seeing fields of dead soldiers to being a Good Humor Man, driving an ice cream truck.

Now, he and the others are suffering from post-traumatic stress disorder.

"A lot of these guys buried themselves in work their whole life, but now that they're retired, they have time to think, to reminisce for the first time," says a clinical social worker who leads the weekly group. "They find themselves becoming more physically disabled. They're losing their friends. And it brings it all back."

They gather each week in Group Therapy Classroom 2 at a Department of Veterans Affairs building in the city where I live, Eugene. It's a barren room, nothing much more than chairs, a grease board, and a box of Kleenexes, which get used for more than nose-blowing.

"Finally, I can talk to someone who understands," says McKee, who fought at the battle of Chosin Reservoir in 1950. In the sub-zero cold of the North Korean mountains, 15,000 U.S. soldiers spent two weeks fighting their way out of a trap set by 120,000 Chinese soldiers.

M*A*S*H it was not. "I know now that hell freezes over," McKee says, "because we were there."

Another member of the therapy group, 65-year-old Mark English, was in Korea, too. After 18 months of war, he returned home. He was so distraught over two men's deaths because of his own negligence that he threw himself in front of a car, which narrowly missed him.

"I blamed myself for causing the deaths of those men," he says.

In 1953, group therapy wasn't hot stuff, so he limped on the best he could. Four marriages. Three divorces. A string of jobs. "I had a tremendous amount of anger," he says.

Finally, a glimmer of hope. In part, he says, because of a recommitment to Christ. In part because of this therapy group that allows him to make sense of a painful past.

"All I know is I love these guys," English says. "We are close and getting closer."

Hershberger, who arrived in France six days after D-Day, was in frontline combat for nearly six months. "Our life expectancy was three weeks," he says.

He likens the therapy sessions to surgery. "It's uncomfortable when it's happening, but once it's over, there's healing."

The others understand when he talks about how a low-flying plane will remind him of a German ME-109. "There's no getting away from it," he says. "But telling this kind of stuff to someone who wasn't there is like you or me telling someone what it's like to have a baby."

The victories in Classroom 2 have been small, but they are victories nevertheless. A sullen World War II vet gradually began warming up, joking, laughing. He would die before the group reached its first anniversary, but everyone remembers the day he told the others he hadn't laughed so long and hard in years.

Then there's McKee, the Marine who walks with a cane because of frostbite suffered at Chosin Reservoir. At Thanksgiving, his family was sitting down to dinner when he announced he had something to say and do.

He talked about how he thought he'd been spared in Korea, in part, to help raise this great family. And how much he loved them. Then he did something nobody had ever seen before: He walked over to his daughters, Mary and Beth, and for the first time ever, gave them each a hug.

To Climb a Tree

IN THE CITY WHERE I LIVE, a local middle school unearthed a time capsule from waaaaaaaay back in 1976, which made me feel really old. Time capsules, I always thought, were supposed to be opened after, say, 100 years and tell you how your great-grandparents' generation lived.

But 1976? That's the year I graduated from college. Reading the article in our newspaper only made me feel older when I discovered the young people were mocking the stuff we valued back then. I didn't mind them mocking plaid pants and paisley shirts and sideburns that looked like the state of Idaho—and were roughly the same size. But one kid's comment really raised my generational hackles.

"Back then," he said, "they didn't have Nintendo. Your fun would be, like, climbing a tree."

Hey, like, there's a lot to be said for climbing trees.

The world would be a better place if parents would encourage their children to spend one hour less per week watching TV or playing Nintendo or surfing the Net and one hour more climbing trees.

You see, the great thing about a tree is that it basically does nothing. Unlike a TV show, it doesn't try to entertain you. Unlike a video game, it doesn't create some imaginary world you need to conquer. Unlike a coach or camp director, it doesn't divide your day into neat, 30-minute intervals.

Instead, kids get to create their own entertainment. They get to turn that tree into anything they want it to be: Mount Everest. Or a "Star Wars" X-Wing Fighter. Or the world headquarters for Students Against Spinach.

OK, I realize that middle-schoolers may be too sophisticated for tree climbing; the important thing is that they be encouraged to use their imaginations. But I don't see it happening much.

Today, some busy parents compensate for their lack of time with their kids by getting them Nintendo, videos, and other stuff with prepackaged imagination. They pack their kids' schedules with programs and clubs and practices—all orchestrated by adults.

An even bigger problem? As parents, we're afraid to let our kids be bored.

"Boredom is the step before imagination," a teacher once told me. "If a kid tells me he's bored, I say to him, 'You're lucky,' because imagination will soon fill the vacuum."

If you've heard Garrison Keillor's "Dog Days of August" sketch, you understand what the teacher means: The story begins with a bored kid lying in the grass. Suddenly, he sees something move: ants. And he wonders: Do ants have cities? Do they see me? Do ants have uncles and aunts or, perhaps, uncles and *people*? From there, he picks up an ant, names him Jim, twirls him in the air and—"Jim, you OK?"—accidentally hurts him. And wonders: Someday, could these guys, because of radiation or something, morph into giants and could Lake Wobegon be full of 30-foot-tall ants, including one named Jim—"a big ant with a bad limp?"

A friend who teaches elementary school tells me that the thing she seldom hears at recess anymore is "let's pretend." Someone else is doing the pretending for our kids. Someone else is providing the imagination, which robs our children of doing that imagining on their own. Thus, our children become responders, not initiators.

Cynics, of course, will point out that imagination is a two-way street; given freedom to create, one child might make a peace crane and another a pipe bomb. I'm not suggesting parents step back and let their kids raise themselves. But as it is, too many are being raised by stuff that plugs in.

When taking walks, I rarely see kids playing outside, period, much less climbing trees. I think back to my time-capsule days—the '50s and '60s—and remember summer nights of hide-and-seek, Tonka-truck roads, and forts made of firewood.

I feel good that my sons founded the Backyard Baseball Association and spent so many summer nights pretending our back yard was a major-league ballpark that just happened to have a towering fir in right-center field.

Do I think we should all kill our TVs and go climb trees? No, but we shouldn't panic when our kids grow bored. Because, when left to their own devices, they're allowed the potential to create something from nothing—and whether that something is a homemade game or a 30-foot-tall ant with a bad limp, there's value in such creating.

Twice Warmed

He who cuts his own wood is twice warmed.

THE SAYING WAS ON THE KITCHEN WALL of a woman I once interviewed...

...near the freezer that was chilling five homemade apple pies...

...in the room next to the old-fashioned wringer washing machine...

...which sits just across from the wood cookstove...

...where she had just finished grilling pancakes made from scratch over a fire fueled by pine gathered by her and her husband.

"I'm just not caught up in modern living," the 64-year-old woman told me, as she kneaded dough for what would be five loaves of bread. "I drag my feet and dig in my heels."

She washed dishes by hand, saying dishwashers wasted water. She did nearly all of her cooking on a woodstove. She even made her own soap.

She warned her three grown children never to give her a microwave oven. "If I don't have time to cook," she said, "then I don't have time to live."

I find something exceedingly rich in that comment: *If I don't have time to cook, then I don't have time to live.*

What the woman was saying, I believe, was something profound about the value of time.

New technology is often sold to us as a time-saver—and certainly that can be a good thing. If my oven can automatically clean itself, then, theoretically, I can spend more time with my family. But there's a more insidious side to technology.

If, as with the automatic oven cleaner, technology can free us up, so also can it enslave us. Consider the photo I clipped from the newspaper, touting a laptop computer: A little boy was fishing while his father sat off by himself, lost in laptop work. What will that little boy remember about the experience? Not that his father took him fishing, but that a computer was more important than he was.

If, as with a cell phone, technology can bring us together, it can also pull us apart. You see, and hear, it happening more wherever you go these days—restaurants, ballparks, everywhere: People's experiences with one another are interrupted by phone calls. I once watched a man and woman eating out; the man spent virtually the entire time on a cell-phone call with someone else. Sad.

If, as with a microwave, technology can cook our food faster, it can also rob us of the experience of the *process* of making food. I think of a couple I know who, each night, make *an experience* out of preparing a dinner together and eating it. You gain no such value from popping something in the microwave.

We are shifting from a process-oriented culture to a results-oriented culture. Strapped for time, we pay a fast-food restaurant to feed our family. We pay a child-care center to nurture our children. Some even pay a store clerk to do their gift shopping.

Lost in the process are people. Relationships. Connections.

One of the most meaningful experiences I had with my father was building a little sailboat with him. He could have bought such a boat. But he chose, instead, to build it with me—and that allowed us, father and son, to work together toward a common goal. There's deep value in that.

When we punch buttons or buy something instead of creating it ourselves, some of that value is lost.

Though I've received many cash Christmas bonuses over the years, I can't remember a single thing I've purchased with those bonuses. But I will never forget the wooden clipboard given to me by an editor one Christmas. Why? Because he had made it himself, specifically for me. It had not been picked up from the five-and-dime on an eleventh-hour shopping spree. It had been custom-crafted with laminated woods, with me in mind.

I wonder if, at times, we don't become that eleventh-hour shopper with our children, with our marriages, with our friends—too content with the five-and-dime when such people deserve more from us.

I think of a friend of mine who handcrafted a wooden hope chest for his daughter. What did that tell her about how much she meant to him?

But as technology advances and the pace of life increases, such personal touches fall by the wayside. I recently encountered my first computerized checkout system in a grocery store. Oh, it did just fine adding up all my items—and was speedy to boot. But I'm a sucker for human interaction—again, that's a big part of why we're *here*—and there is no human interaction in a computerized checkout system.

In his wonderful book *Bowling Alone,* Robert Putnam argues that we've become a lonely people, largely because our connections with each other have plummeted, depleting what he refers to as "social capital"—the value of our social networks. He points out that husbands and wives spend three or four times as much time watching TV together as they spend talking to each other.

"Moreover, as the number of TV sets per household multiplies, even watching together becomes rarer. More and more of our television viewing is done entirely alone."

And more teenagers now have their own televisions, telephones, and computers; gone are the days when being sent to one's room was a punishment. Now, from the teen's perspective, it's a godsend. *Finally!*

So, yes, technology can allow us to accomplish more. But, insidiously, it also pulls us apart—as communities, as families, as husbands and wives. (Did I tell you about the couple I saw walking in front of our house, both with headphones on? Why even bother walking together if conversation isn't going to be part of the deal? I mean, what's the point of taking a walk *together?*)

The baby boomer generation, of course, is nothing if not able to rationalize away just about everything, including lack of time between parents and their children. Thus, in the '80s it invented "quality time" to soothe its guilt over parents not spending "quantity time" with their children. Meanwhile, many of my fellow boomers also compensated for their lack of time commitment by showering their kids with toys and games and computers and TV sets and the latest fad of the moment.

But in the last two decades, it's become clear that what kids really want from parents is this: time. The November 1998 *New York Times* magazine asked kids what they thought was cool about their moms and, surprise, it wasn't that she had an impressive business title or made enough money so they could buy designer clothes. It was that she had time for them.

Out of 15 possible characteristics of the "ideal" mother, having an important job ranked fourteenth. Being at home ranked first. "The coolest mom I know who's not mine is Connor's. She plays soccer with him all the time. I don't think she has a job. She cooks."

So if you're looking for ways to extract yourself from the clutches of materialism, is the answer "quality time," that lingering buzzword from the '80s? Yes and no. Yes, because time with our children should be of first-rank quality. No, because quality time is not enough. If quality time were sufficient, why not use the same concept in schools, businesses, and hospitals? Let's send our children to school only one month a year—but make it a *quality* month. Let's work just one day a week—but let's make it a *quality* day. Let's open the hospital only an hour a day—but let's make it a *quality* hour.

I'm not suggesting we smother our children or spouses with our presence, but either we're there to help meet their needs or they'll find a replacement who will. Relationships take time.

Yes, technology can be a wonderful thing; it can save time, save effort, even save lives. But if we're going to infuse our lives with meaning and purpose, there's no replacement for time with the people we care about.

I once did a story on hospices—places that take care of the dying—and asked the director how volunteers contributed most. It wasn't, she said, their medical knowledge, their ability to lift patients, or even their personalities. It was their willingness to *be there when they were needed.*

Too often we buy into the Great American Edict that if some product is new, it must somehow also be *necessary.* Hey, the world got along fine for centuries without "The Clapper." And, frankly, the woodstove woman seemed far more content—and far more concerned about the meals she was serving others—than plenty of people I've met who had the best microwaves money could buy.

So maybe, like her, we should be a bit more concerned about getting "caught up in modern living." Maybe, rather than assuming that we *must* buy whatever new technological device comes along, we should "drag our feet and dig in our heels" a bit. Because processes are often as important as results.

Take it from someone who has never forgotten building a boat with his father.

A Man of Vision

I WAS A LITTLE DOWN THAT OCTOBER MORNING. So much work, so little time. My youngest son's car was in the shop—again. The ice maker in the fridge was busted. The post-vacation weight I'd lost had been found.

Then I met Forrest Groff. He was the blind man a couple of booths over at a hole-in-the-wall restaurant called Rose's Diner. Walked there a mile every weekday morning with his yellow lab, Texas.

Invited me home to meet the wife. Forrest was 86, Della 88. Married 64 years.

He rambled. But eventually he got to where he was going, and it was well worth the wait.

"My life's motto is 'I will overcome no matter what comes my way,'" he said with I-have-a-dream fervor.

When I left two hours later, all I knew was this: This man was something. And a busted ice maker was nothing.

❨   ❨   ❨

HIS FATHER WAS A DRUNK. He was the oldest, so he took care of the family. Followed migrant camps in Oregon, picking whatever fruit or vegetable needed picking.

Said he got his character from his grandfather in Colorado while helping him farm. Got his faith from the same place after his 8-year-old brother, Orville, was run over by a car. As he lay dying, said Forrest, the boy said two things: that he loved his brothers, even though one of them, Everett, had once poked him in the cheek with a pair of scissors, and that he could see Jesus and was going to go be with him.

Never forgot that. Said "I gave my heart to the Lord" and was baptized in a horse tank at "Moe's barnyard." He was 12.

Returned to Oregon. Did yard work when the migrant season was over. Walked six miles into a town called Newberg each day and six miles back.

Grew in his faith at the Church of the Brethren's Camp Myrtlewood near Myrtle Point, Oregon.

Remembered words of his grandfather: "If something needs doing, do it right; if it needs to be done, do it now; and there's a place for everything."

Decided his place was in Chicago, going to a Church of the Brethren seminary. Hitchhiked there. Met Della on his first Sunday at church; couldn't resist those long braids.

They married in 1936—Depression days—and later moved to Springfield, Oregon, where Rose's Diner is. The seminary wanted him to be the denomination's national church building director, so he attended the University of Oregon's School of Architecture.

They had four kids. At one point, he was pastoring a church, building a house, attending school, working in a cabinet shop, leading a Boy Scout troop, and serving as director of Camp Myrtlewood, all at once. "I've never lived such an exciting life," he said—and meant it.

The flood hit in '45. The Willamette River ruined the family's home. Forrest built a new one. "I'm a stubborn man," he said. "Ever since I took care of my mama and our family, I vowed I wouldn't let my family suffer like that."

Designed some 150 churches; built a dozen. Tried to donate half of all he made to the church.

Retired. Moved to California. Started investing in property. Did well.

Prostate cancer, 1975. Surgery, one of 25 he's had in his life.

Moved to the southern Oregon coast. While building a gift shop in 1981 was walking on the rafters when he realized he couldn't see out of one eye. Glaucoma. Right eye. That's OK, he figured, still have the left.

Was making a ship's wheel on a lathe a year later when a piece of wood shattered and hit his left eye. That's OK, he figured, still have arms and legs.

Moved back to Springfield in 1989. Hit by a car a few years later while walking home from breakfast. Broken leg. Cancer returned in 1997. More surgery.

Then, in 1999, remembered those words of his grandfather. *If it needs to be done, do it now.* Told Della—"my pretty lady"—they should donate money for a new log lodge at Camp Myrtlewood. And design it, too.

But how? she wondered.

We can do it, he said. Together.

He talked. Della drew. And erased. And drew again. And erased. And drew. Six months of this, on and off. "Blood and sweat," said Forrest.

Then, finally, finished. Sent plans to a log lodge company in Idaho, whose president said he had little problem turning them into reality. "A lot of our clients don't understand construction," the company's president said. "Forrest does. We spoke the same language. He had the mental picture." And Della made it a visual picture.

Originally, the lodge was to be called Forest Cove. Forrest liked that, what with his name and all. But then he got a better idea.

Remember what else his grandfather said: *A place for everything.* What about Della, who had been his wife for 64 years and his eyes for nearly 20?

It would, he decided, be called Forest Dell Lodge—the legacy of a man with vision.

Joy of Camping

THE CLOUDS ABOVE SUTTLE LAKE in Oregon's Cascade Mountains were thick and black, like the smoke from burning tires. When you're ten years old and think camping is the greatest thing since the invention of chocolate, you don't want to see a sky like that, particularly on the first day of your family vacation.

So you wait and listen and hope, and then you hear them: those reassuring words from your father.

"Aw, it's just a squall," he says, looking at the charcoal sky. "It'll pass in no time."

My guess is that it passed sometime shortly before my high school graduation. Our family—Mom, Dad, and my older sister Linda—spent that entire weekend sitting under a tarp, listening to the rain fill the plastic and spill to the ground.

We told every knock-knock joke we'd ever heard. We not only read every article in the two dog-eared *Reader's Digest*s we had brought, but the magazine's staff box and Statement of Ownership as well.

Twice. And wouldn't have traded the memory for anything.

My sons are nearly grown and gone now—21 and 18—but in our pre-baseball days, it was camping that linked us to previous generations of our family. Like my parents before me and my father's parents before him, we are woven together by some inexplicable desire to get smoke in our eyes, sit on fishing lures, and offer ourselves as human sacrifices to tribes of bloodthirsty mosquitoes.

Why? It's easy to answer that question when you're watching a full moon reflect on a high-mountain lake or observing a chipmunk steal M&MS or reading Psalms as the wind tickles the branches of the Douglas firs. It's tougher to answer when it's 5 A.M. and you're the only one in the tent not asleep, a tree root is poking you between your shoulder blades, and some guy three camps away is snoring like a chain saw with a bad carburetor.

When my oldest son was four, we had been fishing for days in a small boat when he suddenly, quite philosophically, asked, "Dad, why do we fish?"

He was not concerned about the ethics of the activity, he was perplexed because he had never seen me catch a fish and didn't understand the purpose of our mission. You sat in a boat the size of a bathtub and threw salmon eggs over the side and whispered while your cramped legs went to sleep. What sort of strange ritual was this?

Now, as an adult, I find myself pondering the same question: What sort of strange ritual is this? A father and son fishing. A family camping. Why give up microwave ovens and soft mattresses for eight-foot boats and outhouses that are too far when you need them and too close when you don't?

Part of the reason we camp and fish, I think, is because of the heartfelt utterance of Tevye in *Fiddler on the Roof.* "Tradition!" Ours is a world where traditions are easily trampled. So as parents, we want our children to have the experiences we had as children.

Thus, we go camping—and bring the flashlight whose batteries have been dead since the Carter administration. We forget the can opener and mutilate a can of beef chili stew with a knife. And we use nearly as much blood, sweat, and tears putting up a 12-foot nylon tent as the Egyptians used building the pyramids. Why? Tradition!

Take camp songs. As a boy, I remember groaning as we sat around the fire and my mother broke into songs, including one about how we "love to go a wandering…" Now, I'm the one who breaks into camp songs as my children moan in sweet harmony. Why? Tradition!

Take marshmallows. They make no particular sense. They usually become charred torches with the culinary appeal of coal. And the mushy part inside usually winds up in a child's hair, attracts a weekend's worth of pine needles, and ultimately has to be clear-cut with a pair of scissors. But you *must* roast marshmallows while camping. Why? Tradition!

Why else do we camp? Because it brings us face to face, not only as tent sardines but as human beings. At home, too often we gather around the TV, each of us reacting to it, not to each other. High in the mountains, we gather around a fire, which draws us to each other and not to itself.

Never mind that the same fire, before the weekend is out, will melt the toe of at least one son's tennis shoe and spew ashes into someone else's hot chocolate. It will also stir memories, prompt small talk, and as the evening deepens and the embers glow more faintly, gently nudge us into big talk.

Amid a world in technological overdrive, camping brings us back to the basics. At home, our imaginations are rendered nearly useless by computers and videos and gadgets and gizmos. In the woods, we're forced to use our creativity. To improvise. To work together as a team. To figure out how to get Mom's sunglasses off the bottom of the lake, 12 feet down.

We learn things while camping—not only about how to whittle a hot-dog stick but, say, what it means to be honest. Once, while I was fishing with my father, people in nearby boats had caught their legal limits but continued to catch more. When my father and I reached our limit, he started the motor (sixteenth pull), and we headed for shore. Though such things may seem insignificant at the time, sons remember them: Honesty was something to be valued.

We create memories that, in a sense, validate the vision— that say to us, over and over, *human connections are good.*

From my own boyhood, I remember the time we were asleep in the tent when our dog Jet started barking wildly, bothered by something in our camp. My mother was sure it was a bear. I was thinking Bigfoot, rumored to prowl the Cascades. In fact, it was my father's underwear, hanging on a clothesline, eerily silhouetted in the light of a full moon.

As we grow from children to adults, we tuck such memories away and forget them, like photographs stowed in an attic. But every now and then, we remember the feel of piercing the cool water with a swan dive, the smell of bacon and eggs on a Coleman stove, the sound of an ax splitting the evening's firewood. And we try to allow our children to feel and smell and hear those same things.

It isn't important that we have the perfect experience while camping. Or that we're Super Campers, whose boat motors always start on the first pull and whose air mattresses never go flat in the night. What matters is that we spend time communicating with each other, communicating with God, and enjoying the amazing creation of His.

What's important is simply being together, as my family was at a campground called Denny Creek, back when the boys were much smaller. The thunder sounded as if we were beneath a celestial bowling alley, and the rain was pelting our tent. My sons looked at me, seeking reassurance. What I told them marked a rite of passage for me, from son to father.

"Aw, it's just a squall," I said. "It'll pass in no time."

Part III

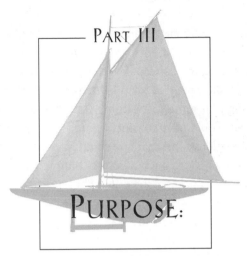

Purpose:

Understanding Your Voyage

The rudder serves two purposes, to initiate major changes in direction and to provide increased resistance to sideways slip at the back of the boat.

The Handbook of Sailing

IT'S A BLUSTERY FALL DAY, THE CRANKY SKIES spitting occasional raindrops as if to signal worse things to come. But on a residential street, the woman's flower stand is open as usual, offering the world a smidgen of sunshine.

Seven days a week, 52 weeks a year, her homegrown flowers sit on the tattered card table outside her house. Chrysanthemums, zinnias, baby's breath, and more, all bunched in coffee cans. Two bucks a bundle. Just leave your money on the table— or put it in the fishing creel on the porch.

A little short this week? Take the flowers. At 86, the woman who toils in the garden to produce them isn't out to get rich, just to pay for her fertilizer and perhaps a few root-beer floats for her grandsons.

She is from a different generation than mine. In her simplicity and selflessness, she represents the flip side to us baby boomers, who have elevated the concept of self to new and dangerous heights. In her daily routine from garden to card table, it's as if she were caught in some sort of time warp, blindly settling for so little when she could have so much more.

Didn't she understand that she could have maximized her profits by selling bulk to a wholesaler? That with a computer and the right software package, she could have streamlined her operation, boosting her net intake?

No, she did not, nor did she want to. What she understood was this: "The people who buy my flowers are happy," she told me. "And that makes me happy."

In other words, in her own simple way, the woman had embraced the biblical concept that it *is* more blessed to give than to receive. And in doing so, she was fulfilling a *purpose*.

Why Are We Doing What We're Doing?

If we're to live more meaningful lives, we not only need to realize where we are and envision where we need to get. We also need to understand why we need get there. Otherwise, we're ships without rudders, going wherever the wind may blow us.

When Robin Graham took his bearings and envisioned his voyage, he did so because he perceived a certain pointlessness in his life. And though he would ultimately realize that his lack of purpose went deeper than he originally thought, at the time he saw his round-the-world trip as fulfillment of what was lacking.

His motive, he would later tell reporters, was neither personal glory nor adventure, but something far deeper—as if it were something he'd been born to do. He referred to a line from Shakespeare's *Hamlet:* "There's a divinity that shapes our ends, rough-hew them how we will."

If what's really important is relationships, then we would be wise to heed the divinity that shapes our ends. And wise to examine some of the baby-boomer philosophies that have guided so many of us. Simply put, you can't live for God and others if you believe you were put on earth to receive instead of give, to heed the '60s generation anthem to "do your own thing," to follow the TV commercials and make choices because "I'm worth it." Relationships don't work that way, *won't* work that way.

If the baby boom generation had a "first hero," it was President John F. Kennedy, whose death is apparently seared into a generation's collective memory more deeply than his life. "Ask not what your country can do for you," he exhorted, "but what you can do for your country."

The call exhorted people to sacrifice, to put the collective good above self. But somewhere along the way, the boomers lost their sense of purpose. Remember, this was the all-you-need-is-love generation, the generation that disdained both materialism and the over-30 crowd that, in their eyes, had sold out to it.

Instead, we became a generation that asked not what we could do for our country, but what our country could do for us. What our spouse could do for us. What our church could do for us. What God could do for us.

In the '70s, self-gratification became the goal for many. A Rutgers University poll showed that while 41 percent of the public at large felt that "doing the things that offer personal satisfaction and pleasure" were more important than "working hard and doing what is expected," 67 percent of boomers felt that way.

After a decade of searching for self, in the '80s boomers tried to find their identity in work. A large segment embraced the corporate world with vigor. On the outside, it looked like a nose-to-the-grindstone, duty-bound work ethic. But at its core was ego. The ultimate goal was not some selfless attempt to put bread on the table or loyally serve the company, but to climb higher. To be noticed. To *be* somebody. Work, in essence, became the idol of a generation.

The all-you-need-is-love generation became the all-you-need-is-bucks generation, our materialistic cravings spawning catalogs filled with flashy-but-meaningless toys, outlet malls lined with trendy fashions, and therapy offices lined with lots of needy patients. By the late '80s, boomers were ten times more likely to be depressed than their parents or grandparents and five times as likely to be divorced, according to *Psychology Today*. Nearly half of more than 4,000 male executives categorized their lives as "empty and meaningless," according to one study.

Lost in boomers' pursuit of the American Dream instead of God's will—which is relationships—was something of overwhelming importance: meaning.

The newspaper where I work recently asked people to explain the meaning of life. The answers were diverse, but most were tinged with an obvious sense of futility.

"Many years ago, back in my college days when I was young and idealistic, I had all sorts of thoughts about the meaning of life, and it was really a big issue to me," wrote one person. "Over the years, I have decided there really is no meaning. We're just here."

These are words from someone sailing a rudderless voyage, someone who may well know Thoreau's "quiet desperation." And what, really, is quiet desperation? It's an acute sense of lack of purpose, as if we don't really matter, as if we're predestined to live just a dog-eat-dog life where personal survival reigns supreme. Perhaps that explains the popularity of TV's *Survivors;* surviving, not living abundant lives, has become our one pathetic goal—no wonder so many relate to the show.

Having personally survived Nazi death camps, a man named Viktor Frankl studied what it was that allows some people to retain their humanity in inhumane circumstances. In essence, he found that it went beyond intellect or psychology. It was *meaning*—the ability to find purpose in what we do, no matter how insignificant the task might seem.

"Being human," he wrote, "means relating and being directed to something or someone other than oneself."

The Craving for Riches

When we try to fill our emptiness with something other than what it was intended to be filled with—with riches instead of relationships—we're doomed. That was clear long before the first boomer bought a BMW.

"People who want to get rich," wrote the Apostle Paul to Timothy, "fall into temptation and a trap and into many foolish and harmful desires that plunge men into ruin and destruction. For the love of money is a root of all kinds of evil. Some people, eager for money, have wandered from the faith and pierced themselves with many griefs" (1 Timothy 6:9-10).

In the Gospels of Matthew, Mark, and Luke, Jesus doesn't mince words about wealth. He warns that it can become a false god, that it can create a false sense of security, that it can, in essence, replace our dependence on Him.

But oh, how that money tempts us—and always has. While in Skagway, Alaska, I learned about the Klondike Gold Rush near the end of the nineteenth century. Skagway, a port town, was where some 100,000 people flocked to so they could begin their journeys to strike it rich. They endured a 3,600-foot high, snowy mountain pass with 60-pound packs on their back and 550 miles by boat to get to the Canadian Yukon. Thousands died in the process. Few actually hit pay dirt. Indeed, the most lasting legacy of the Klondike Gold Rush wasn't what people found, it was what they lost—in many cases their lives.

Though more diffused and less dramatic, today's stories of people madly pursuing their money dreams are no less real—or destructive. A man who works at a 70-hour-a-week job—and sacrifices his family in the process—is no less driven than a man who gave up his family to struggle for gold in 1897. And a woman hooked on the QVC channel who places her weekly orders with a cordless phone, Visa card, and 1-800 number is no less addicted to *stuff* than a woman lugging a 60-pound pack over White Pass.

Russian author Leo Tolstoy tells the story of a peasant who is offered all the land he can walk around in a day. The man hurries to get around as much as possible, his exertion so great that he falls dead just as he gets back to where he had begun. He ends up with nothing.

When we strive for the wrong things in life, what we ultimately come up with is nothing. Meanwhile, we miss much along the way as our lives become complicated and cluttered by the stuff that we thought was treasure but we actually find is trivial.

Like other addictions, the craving to have more money and more stuff is never satisfied. It always wants more. Consider the stock-market maniac whose cell phone seems surgically attached to his ear. Consider gamblers who rarely can quit, even when winning. Consider how quickly, like some sort of drug, the high of a new purchase wears off and we desperately seek another hit.

We can laugh at the "Live to Shop" bumper stickers, but sadly, there's more truth in those words than some of us would want to admit.

Likewise, in the book of Luke we read the parable of the rich fool, who dreamed of building bigger and bigger barns so he could eat, drink, and be merry. Meanwhile, he missed the bigger picture of what life is all about.

"Stones and Sea," a song by the Celtic band Eden's Bridge, says it well: We begin by looking for stones on the beach, some pretty, some not, and after spending much time collecting them, we're finally inspired to raise our eyes to the glory of the sea itself—which we missed during all those years of gathering stones.

It's easy, of course, to point fingers at others who spend their lives gathering stones. It's easy to shake our heads at, say, baseball's

Sammy Sosa bemoaning his $10.5-million-a-year contract that doesn't give him "the kind of long-term security" he thinks he needs. Or at singer Elton John, who testified in a court case that he spends as much as $2.15 million to live—per *month*.

It's harder to look at ourselves in the mirror, where we must not only face who we are but *why* we've become that person. Jesus challenges us to consider not only our actions, but our motives.

> Jesus sat down opposite the place where the offerings were put and watched the crowd putting their money into the temple treasury. Many rich people threw in large amounts. But a poor widow came and put in two very small copper coins, worth only a fraction of a penny.
>
> Calling his disciples to him, Jesus said, "I tell you the truth, this poor widow has put more into the treasury than all the others. They all gave out of their wealth; but she, out of her poverty, put in everything—all she had to live on."
>
> —Mark 12:41-44

Finding Purpose by Being a Servant

In a world that can be headstrong and haughty, we're called to live humbly, to live from the heart. In a stress-for-success world, we're called not to be "successes," but servants.

"Even the Son of Man did not come to be served, but to serve, and to give his life as a ransom for many" (Mark 10:45).

Therein lies what we were created for—to love God with all our heart, soul, and mind, and to love our neighbor as ourself. Therein lies the essence of meaning. Therein lies the rudder of our voyage: to serve.

Our highest calling is to make sacrifices for God and others, which produces in us something far more meaningful than comfort. It produces character. But such character can't grow if we wrap ourselves in a materialistic cocoon and never touch anyone; neither can it grow if we run away to the woods and refuse to be touched.

If that means a challenging voyage—and it does—we must understand that's a necessary part of the journey. Character grows best in the winds of discomfort, in taking a risk and challenging oneself. It's the same way an athlete gets stronger, quicker, and more coordinated—he or she has to find resistance: a lap to run, a barbell to lift, a lap to swim.

So it is on our voyage. Sailboats, author James Michener writes, do poorly when the wind is directly behind them. "What is needed is a wind slightly opposed to the ship, for then tension can be maintained and juices can flow and ideas can germinate, for ships, like men, respond to challenge."

We live in a world where money, power, and prestige blow from directly behind us and can easily give us the sense that we're getting where we need to get. But Michener is right. A sailboat does poorly when the wind is directly behind it. And so it is with people on a downwind tack.

Challenge requires tension. Pursuing good things requires tension. Risk requires tension. A guitar plays beautiful music because of tension. Growth doesn't happen without tension.

We must allow God to stretch us. And a significant way we can be stretched is in building relationships, where our deepest purpose lies.

Fulfilling that purpose may be as ambitious as giving up a lucrative medical practice and moving to a Third World country to treat the poor, which a teammate of mine on a medical mission trip to Haiti did. It may be as bold as rededicating ourselves to a spouse. Or it may be as simple as putting flowers on a tattered card table in front of our house, just for people to enjoy.

Regardless of how such a purpose might play out, it must begin—as it did with Robin Graham—in seeking the "divinity that shapes our ends, rough-hew them how we will."

The Silent Hero

ONE AFTERNOON LAST WEEK, the sky above the city where I live was scattered with hundreds of balloons, like multicolored cake sprinkles—red, yellow, black, and white. They were released in honor of a 96-year-old woman who had requested them for her memorial service, not to celebrate *her*, but to celebrate the children from around the world. To celebrate, as the song says, that

> *Jesus loves the little children,*
> *All the children of the world,*
> *Red and yellow, black, and white...*

That's really what Bertha Holt's life was all about—God's children:

The little girl in Korea left on a doorstop by a mother who felt someone else could do what she could not.

The little boy herded onto the last plane leaving Saigon in 1975.

The baby in India who never knew a mother or a father.

Thanks to Bertha and Harry Holt—founders of Holt International Children's Services, which is based in Eugene, Oregon—such children got a second chance in life. That, I realize in pondering the woman's life, was her real legacy.

Oh, you could point to her two-page list of honors, the latest being a Kiwanis award whose earlier recipients include no less than Mother Teresa. She once shared grandmother stories with the Queen Mother of England. And upon her death, she was honored at the highest levels.

You could also point to her energy. She rose daily at 5:30 A.M. to pray. Until the week before she died, she drove an old vw bus, and flew so often that she was up and down more than the stock market. While in her 70s, she trained for visits to missionaries in high-altitude countries by huffing to the top of nearby Spencer Butte while carrying a backpack loaded with rocks. And at 92, she set a national 400-meter age group record in a Masters track meet.

But Bertha Holt's real legacy, I realize, isn't found in her honors or energy. It's found in the people whose lives she touched.

People such as Mare-Lee Vance, adopted out of Seoul, South Korea in 1961 and now, at 43, the director for academic support and advising services at George Mason University in Fairfax, Virginia.

"Had Bertha and Harry Holt not come along, I'd probably be screwing in light bulbs at some city-sponsored shelter, with a bowl of rice as my ration," said Vance, who earned a doctorate from Michigan State in 1994.

She still has the handwritten letter of congratulations from Bertha Holt that arrived after graduation: "Dear Dr. Vance," it begins, and ends with, "...may the Lord bless your work. Grandma Holt."

People such as Brian Hester, adopted out of South Vietnam in 1974 and now, at 27, a house painter in Columbus, Ohio.

"The Holts played a huge part in my life. I got a second chance. Without them, I'd probably be back in Vietnam. Probably dead."

He's now engaged to be married, and he and his fiancée have already decided to not only have children, but to adopt a child.

"There are only a few people you can label as heroes in life, and I'd label Bertha Holt as one," he said. "There are sports heroes and entertainment heroes, but Bertha Holt is what I'd call a silent hero. A lot of people are surviving today because of what she and her husband did behind the scenes long ago."

What they did, really, was see a need and fill it. Shortly after the end of the Korean War, Bertha and her husband, Harry, took a huge step of faith. Felt God calling and answered. Took a risk and were blessed by it.

She and Harry were simple Willamette Valley farmers—poor in money but rich in faith—who, in their 50s, were deeply moved when seeing a film about the thousands of Korean-American orphans left in the wake of the war.

Unbeknownst to one another, each felt a tug from God that said, *Adopt some of those orphans.* But how? And how many? Bertha prayed and sensed that the number was eight. But she wasn't sure how committed to the idea Harry was, so when he asked how many she thought they should adopt, she said six.

Harry then confided he had another number in mind. "I was thinking more like eight," he said.

They scraped together what money they had, and Harry flew to Korea to follow the couple's vision. At the time, the Holts' actions were nothing short of revolutionary. Inter-country adoption was rare in the 1950s and was given the cold shoulder by the social work establishment. The common prac-tice was to match children and adoptive parents by back-ground and color, which helped conceal the adoption.

But the Holts believed children were children—and what they needed, above all, was parents to love them, regardless of color or culture. It took five months and—quite literally—an Act of Congress, but in October 1955, the Holts became parents of eight adopted children.

The Holts, through their compassion and perseverance, helped put a new face on international adoption. They showed the world that adoption was not a badge of shame but a sign of love.

When the media caught wind of the story, the Holts were swamped by calls and letters from people around the country. How could they adopt these children? Thus was Holt Interna-tional Children's Services founded.

When Harry died of a heart attack in 1964, some thought the agency would close. Bertha Holt wasn't among them. "This work was always God's work," she said. "If He wanted it to continue, it would."

And continue it did. By the time Bertha Holt died on July 31, 2000, more than 50,000 children from more than a dozen countries had found homes through Holt International.

People such as Asha Gayatri Noah, adopted from an orphanage in Pune, India, and one of the youth leaders in the nondenominational church I attend.

And people such as Russell Lawton, airlifted out of Saigon on the last flight out in April 1975 and now a second-grade teacher in Omaha, Nebraska.

"The chances of my still being alive, had I not been adopted, would be about one in a million," Lawton said. "I was a sick baby. Malnutrition. I weighed four-and-a-half pounds at five months."

He was adopted by a family in Grand Island, Nebraska, recently met a Korean ballet dancer from New York—also adopted through Holt—and hopes to be married soon.

"We are the new adoptees of our culture," he said. "People who look at us see us as Asian or Vietnamese or Korean, but they don't know our stories. When Bertha passed on, we became the ones who will carry on what she and her husband began."

Death always stings. And yet I'm not sure that I've seen a life so well lived, so purposefully lived, so humbly lived, as the one lived by Bertha Holt.

For those who believe they're too old or too poor or too alone to contribute anything meaningful to the world, Bertha Holt's life argues otherwise.

A few days after her memorial service, which was held only a few miles from my house, I was walking back from our mailbox when I saw it lying on the ground: a popped yellow balloon, string still attached to its neck.

I picked it up, placed it on a shelf in my office, and smiled to myself. It was as if the heavens had air-mailed me a reminder from someone whose legacy lives on. And the reminder was this:

They are precious in His sight...

The Waiting Room

A FEW YEARS BEFORE MY FATHER DIED, he needed open-heart surgery. As my mother and I talked in the hospital waiting room, something dawned on me: I've always felt closest to this woman while in hospitals.

Not surprisingly, we first met in one.

When I was 23, she nearly died in one, following an automobile accident.

Now here we were again—mother and son alone, awaiting the fate of the third person in this parent-child triangle.

Hospitals force us to stop and consider all the stuff that gets cast aside in lives driven by deadlines and Day-Timers: Life. Death. And how much we mean to each other.

Hospitals don't allow you to simply glance at your watch and keep running. They demand you pause and consider the whole concept of time and age and change.

Sitting in the waiting room, I found myself thinking not only about my father, but my mother, too. Because hospitals bring me back to that night in 1977 when I saw the red "Emergency" sign and realized, for once, the sign was meant for me. After being involved in an automobile accident, my mother was inside those walls, fighting to live.

Now, in this eddy of anxiety almost two decades later, the two of us had a rare opportunity to simply talk. No turkey to fix. No grandchildren to pull off the ceiling. No agendas to follow.

"I can't believe how young the surgeon is," she said. "We've got Doogie Howser as our doctor."

The man trying to prolong my father's life was 37. I did some quick calculations.

"Mom," I said, "if I have heart surgery when I'm Dad's age and it's done by a 37-year-old doctor, do you realize how old that doctor is now?"

"How old?"

"Seven," I said. "He's a first-grader."

She laughed.

As morning shifted to afternoon, we talked of my father's desire to get out of the hospital and get back to work on his sailboat. Of my sister's latest novel.

We talked of life for me at 40, trying to find balance amid the chaos of commitments. Of life for my mother at 67, looking forward to retiring as a secretary in Oregon State University's political science department.

We said the kind of things that probably wouldn't get said over a Mother's Day lunch or on a long-distance phone call.

"It's interesting," she said, "how mothers and grown daughters talk with each other like this, but mothers and grown sons rarely do."

We talked. We read. We mused.

Seven years old. A first-grader.

I remembered being there once, long ago. My mother, I figure, would have been 34. What do I remember of me? What do I remember of this woman who helped me *become* me?

I remember her pointing to the night sky above Draper Court at a post-Sputnik satellite.

I remember her scolding and comforting me after, for reasons beyond me, I'd thrown a handful of gravel at a passing convertible as a five-year-old and was sure I was going to be hauled off to jail.

I remember her loading up the volleyball gear to drive to the migrant camp, as she did once a week in the summer, as part of a community group that offered the workers a spice of fun in an otherwise grueling week.

Now, she stood beside the man she'd been married to for 48 years. She cried. She had never seen him unconscious and attached to an octopus of tubes and wires.

But Doogie Howser did his job well. My father was fine. In five days, he was ready to go home.

Experiences like this, I've learned, place little pieces in the puzzles that ultimately comprise our lives. The time in that waiting room was not a huge piece, but it was an important piece, drawing a mother and son closer together as they awaited the fate of a man they both loved.

Outside our house, where mom had been staying, we parted. I shook hands with my father and told him, *no bungee jumping.* I hugged my mother goodbye and said little.

It had already been said, back in the hospital, where hearts are broken and mended but never come out quite the same.

The Birthday Gift

LAST WEEK I FOUND INSPIRATION in the buffet line of an all-you-can-eat Chinese restaurant.

It began with an e-mail from a man I'd known in another time and place—a man named Dave Douglass, who had been an associate pastor at a church my family had attended 20 years ago. His father, who lived in the same community I did, was turning 90 years old. The family was coming from all points around the state to honor him. His father and mother had read and enjoyed some books I'd written.

Would I be willing to swing by during the lunch and present an autographed copy of *Where Roots Grow Deep* to him? If you don't mind, he said, could you please inscribe it: "To a couple who has made sure the roots are deep and the tree strong."

I was happy to do so. I felt honored. The restaurant was within two miles of the newspaper where I worked. And I had no schedule conflicts.

Truth be known, I was also feeling a little sorry for Dave. He and his wife had spent more than a decade pastoring a little church in Eastern Oregon, the state's sagebrush outback. Now, he had accepted a new challenge of moving back to the Willamette Valley to become a "church planter." An e-mail updated me with his new adventure:

> *I never dreamed I would be a church planter. I've never done it before. It's a brand new concept to me. Our support is only partially underwritten by [a particular church organization] so we must raise additional support. Instead of being in the position of helping to lend support, I will*

now be the person seeking it. (A significant role reversal!) I am going to a church that doesn't exist. My workplace will be at the park, soccer field, little league games, coffee shop…wherever people are.

They will not come to me. I must go to them. So I enter this ministry with honest fear and trembling because it is totally uncharted waters for me. On the other hand, I move ahead with great confidence because of my confidence in God's leading. This is God's work. What will result in [this new place] is not about me, it's about Him!

At this man's age, most people are retiring. Worried not about planting churches but about harvesting social security benefits. Not hanging around parks and soccer fields but hanging around RV parks and time-share condominiums.

I tried to imagine what it would be like, at age 60, to uproot yourself from the longtime security of a place and move to an unknown place to start a church. I understood why the man felt fear.

The day before the birthday event, I got an e-mail from Dave:

I hate to admit this, but I've been telling my wife for the last two weeks, "I have to be sure and get that check off to Bob!" whereupon I did not do it. This morning she asked me about "the check for Bob."

It's in the mail as I speak or write. I even thought about just giving it to you tomorrow but was quite sure I'd forget. So it's on its way.

On my way to the restaurant I grew a tad apprehensive. I was already feeling bad for the guy; I worried that this might wind up being one of those seemed-like-a-good-idea-at-the-time events that, with aging parents and wild great-grandchildren in a busy restaurant, might make me feel even worse for him.

He greeted me with a broad smile and grip so firm I almost winced—not the man who'd asked me to come but the man's 90-year-old father, the man whose birthday was being celebrated.

"What a surprise to see you here," he said, and reintroduced me to his wife, whom I'd met years ago.

I looked around. Tucked into the corner of the restaurant were four generations of the Douglass family. A little boy walked up to me.

"Are you the writer guy?" he asked.

"Yeah, I guess I am."

"Glad to meet you," he said and shook my hand.

I just stood there and smiled. I looked around and realized there was something different about this family. There was a certain levity in this room. People were talking and laughing as if this weren't just some pain-in-the-neck obligation, but as if they really wanted to be here—not the sense you get among many American families these days. And yet, to a person, they were quick to stop and welcome a guest.

One of the kids spilled his drink. Nobody flared in anger. Nobody chastised the kid. Two people simply mopped up the spill. Outside, the world raced by in a mad rush. But these people seemed to be more interested in each other—and me—than in rushing anywhere.

I signed the book and presented it to the 90-year-old man, who seemed touched by the gift. Then I glanced toward the exit; I had work to do.

"Would you care to join us?" said my friend Dave.

I glanced at the exit, then back at the family.

"I'd love to," I said.

As we went through the buffet line, Dave thanked me over and over for coming. I asked about his position. He sketched in some details that the e-mails had not.

"The truth is, I've never made as little money as I'm making now," he said. "And the truth is, I've never been so excited about doing God's work."

As we were eating, my friend flagged down a waitress. "Ma'am," he whispered, thinking I couldn't hear, "on our bill, you need to make that 23 lunches, not 22. We've added one more."

When I got home from work that night, amid the mail come-ons for credit cards and refinance programs that promised to "Help Your Dreams Come True," I found a $10 check from Dave for the book.

I looked at it. I thought about a man who wanted to honor his 90-year-old father for having "made sure the roots are deep and the tree strong." About 23 lunches instead of 22. About the vision and courage it takes to give up a secure job to sail into uncharted waters.

His father didn't need me for inspiration, I realized; the inspiration was already there, in the man's son.

I folded the check twice and ripped it once.

The $7.1 Million Advance

I STARED AT THE NEWSPAPER HEADLINE, the kind of headline that, as an upstart author, I never dreamed I'd see. But this was no dream. It was right there in the business section of my city's newspaper for all my family and friends to see:

Welch Being Paid Huge Book Advance

Huge as in $7.1 million. Enough money to pay off our mortgage and then some. Enough money to pay for that new middle school/high school building at our church. Enough money to—suddenly, like an Olympic sprinter, my mind was off and running about what I could do with that $7.1 million.

Upgrade my University of Oregon football tickets; for years, I'd been on the 1 yard-line. Now I could take a skybox suite; they're only $45,000 a year. In a few months, I'd find that much change between my sofa cushions. Goodbye hot dogs; hello beef Wellington!

Replace my '91 pickup, the one with the driver-side door that, before I bought it, got caught in an east Texas windstorm and busted the catch-latch so that when you open it, it keeps opening until nearly hitting my left front blinker.

Remodel my house. Better yet, buy a new one. Out in the country. A house with an actual office in it that I don't have to share with my wife the crafter or my son the computer-football player. An office lined with walnut shelves for all my books, organized according to their individual Library of Congress classification numbers, all computerized, of course. No more traipsing out to the carport on cold winter nights to check out that quote in Yancey's *What's So Amazing About*

Grace? I might even put in a bar-code system so that when I loan books to people, my computer will automatically e-mail the borrowers an overdue notice. (If anyone reading this is the person I loaned Jane Kirkpatrick's *A Gathering of Finches* to, please return it. No questions asked.)

I stared at the "Huge Book Advance" headline. Wow. Unbelievable.

If only it were me. If only it were me and not *Jack* Welch, the chairman of GE, "the leading management revolutionary of the century," according to *Fortune* magazine.

In the ten years since my first book, *More to Life Than Having It All*, came out, I've done lots of thinking about the plight of an author. I've thought a lot about how easy it is to look at people like Jack Welch and consider yourself an utter failure. A loser. A nobody.

I remember when I first walked into a bookstore after *More to Life* came out, absolutely stoked to see my book on the shelf—but it took me five minutes to find it because it was hidden behind a life-size cutout of former Texas Rangers pitcher Nolan Ryan. *But he's no author,* I wanted to protest; he just happens to have a 100-MPH fastball and streets named after him and soup commercials starring him; I mean, what has the guy ever written, other than his autograph?

I remember asking a friend and his wife out to dinner to celebrate my first royalty check—then laughing as we realized that the check wouldn't cover the entire meal; I remember showing up at an out-of-town book signing in which only a handful of people, including a trio of girls from the same church I attended, showed up. I thanked them for coming.

"That's OK," one of them said. "We were just killing time while waiting for our ride."

Sigh.

One day I was bemoaning the fact that my book *A Father for All Seasons* was not selling as well as other books; on the

Amazon.com web site, where millions of books are sold, I was ranked 234,903rd. Nobody wants to put a bumper sticker on their car that says that I'M NUMBER 234,903! Instead, they want a bumper sticker that says I'M NUMBER ONE! Nobody even remembers Olympic runners-up, much less folks with six-digit book rankings.

I'm a loser, I said to myself.

My first act of rationalization—instead of comparing myself with the 234,902 books ranked *above* mine—was comparing myself with the millions of books ranked *below* mine. In that light I was, my calculations determined, ranked in the top few percent, since Amazon lists some four million books. That's good, I suggested.

Hey, I'm actually a winner, I said to myself.

But later that day, sifting through e-mail messages, I read one that made me realize I was wrong on both accounts. It was from a soon-to-be father in Pennsylvania who said my book had inspired him to appreciate what an important step he was about to take. To understand what a privilege fatherhood was. To, in essence, realize where his boat was in life, where he needed to sail to, and why he needed to sail there.

"Above all, I think your book has helped remind me that I will not be the be-all and end-all of my son's life. I am simply an instrument through which God draws a little life to Himself."

Reading those words, I was humbled. Humbled to be reminded that, at the deepest level, what validates us is not huge advances or sales figures or rankings or job titles or annual incomes or awards or any other artificial indicator. At the deepest level, what validates us—beyond our validation from God for simply *being*—is the difference we make in the lives of others.

In 1999, *A Father for All Seasons* won the national Gold Medallion award for family and parenting; I was honored.

Humbled that someone thought this book was the best of its kind published the previous year. But again, what matters isn't a wooden plaque on my office wall; what matters is whether my book connects with those who read it.

Slowly, I'm doing better dealing with the so-called success or failure of my books—four so far. I've learned that comparing ourselves to others—be the subject book sales or house size or income level—is, in itself, a lose-lose proposition. Whether we deem ourselves to be "better" or "worse" than someone else, we do so based on a man-made criterion that, like so much of American culture, misses the bigger picture— that assumes what matters most is quantity, not quality—that is all about numbers, not meaning.

Which isn't to say that I don't still struggle when, say, I see a book like 1,000 *Stupid Things People Actually Said* outselling my books ten to one. But I'm learning to see beyond what I used to see. And I'm reminding myself to leaven the disappointments with humor.

Like the time I was returning from having spoken at a writers' conference in California. I had had a box of 40 books—*A Father for All Seasons*—shipped to the conference site; 12 sold. Thus, as I hurriedly packed to catch a flight home, I had to decide whether to have the 28 hardback books shipped home—how humiliating, having to pay twice for their not selling once—or somehow cram them in my suitcase. How humiliating, period.

The airport van was waiting. Pride won out. I madly started stuffing books everywhere I could. Disaster: The suitcase wouldn't close. I threw it on the bed and jumped on it like a crazy man wrestling an alligator, finally getting it zipped shut. The suitcase looked nine months pregnant—with twins.

"Careful," I told the guy at baggage check-in at San Francisco International, "it's *real* heavy."

"Well, I've handled a few heavy bags in my day so I wouldn't—"…he grimaced like a man who'd just had an anvil dropped on his foot—"Man, whatchya got in here, *bricks?*"

"Books."

"Seventy-pound limit," he said, setting it on the scale.

Limit? I hadn't realized there was such a thing.

The orange digitized numbers zipped to 71.5 and stopped.

He looked at me. I looked at him.

He raised his eyebrows slightly. I smiled.

"So, uh, you look like a father," I said. "Wanna few books?"

Pilgrimage to the Past

WHEN OUR CHILDREN WERE YOUNG, I remember the pull of home for Sally and me when the holidays came. I remember the lone time we weren't able to make it home for Thanksgiving and hearing the familiar voices in the background of the long-distance phone call. One of my sister's twins was laughing. My father was taking orders for sandwiches. And my Grandpa Schu was talking—what else?—fresh produce.

In a few minutes, the phone call came to an end. "Happy Thanksgiving," my mother said. "We miss you."

I said goodbye. And the line went dead.

Never is the tug of home so strong as when you hang up following a holiday phone call. What is it about this magnetic force of family?

At Thanksgiving and Christmas, it pulls stronger than at any other time of the year. It's not that way for everybody, I know. Some find their strongest bonds in friends, not family. For others, looking back is simply too painful. And others have no home to return to.

But some of us find ourselves in a paradoxical pattern: Physically, we grow up and leave home; emotionally, we grow up and never leave home. Not really.

We brashly march off to college, smug in our newfound independence. Two weeks later, we're sitting in a closet-sized dorm room, counting the days until Thanksgiving as our stomachs do battle with cafeteria food.

We graduate and hitch our U-Hauls to a star, following jobs wherever they might lead. But we come back every time we unpack the handed-down Christmas tree ornaments or see a home-state license plate.

We establish traditions at a home of our own. But while worthy in themselves, they are offsprings of something deeper—reasonable facsimiles, but not yet the real thing. Like an astronaut's view of the earth, the past gets more intriguing the farther away you get.

So, if possible, we return, and probably not as simply as traveling over the river and through the wood to grand-mother's house. The fact is, regardless of where we live, most of us are from somewhere else, sometimes somewhere else far away.

Many of us are refugees who came to a new place for a new future but are inextricably linked to our pasts. It doesn't matter whether it's California or one of the Carolinas, the homeland pulls.

It is a subtle, unseen pull, like the moon tugging the tides. And just as the ebbs and flows of the oceans become cycles of coming and going, so do our lives. Each day, in our routine reading of the newspaper, we check the temperatures back home. We imagine what, say, 32 degrees would be like there in November. How it would feel.

Each change of season, we picture what it would look like back home. A friend of mine has bookmarked his Ohio home-town's Web page and, every now and then, calls it up to see a remote-camera shot of the local college—just to keep tabs on how it looks decades later.

And if possible, each holiday season we get the neighbors to feed the cats, and we make a pilgrimage to our past.

When we return, we're sometimes reminded less of how the place has changed than of how *we* have changed—some for the better, some for the worse. Scrapbooks bring back the good memories; trips home bring back them all.

But it's good to remember. Not to mire ourselves in the past, but to learn from it, to use it as a reference point. When we look at the dismantled theater stage, we sometimes discover that while making the journey from childhood to adulthood, we discarded some things we shouldn't have. And brought along some baggage we should have left behind.

If the past has been painful, we search the prickly vine for the edible berries.

We dust off treasured traditions, such as the three-generation street-football game followed immediately by mass moaning and groaning from one of the generations.

We renew relationships, or at least search for a smidgen of common ground with the cousin-in-law we haven't seen in five years.

We honor the heritage of family that time and distance have diluted but not destroyed.

Home is not an airbrushed haven manufactured by Hallmark. Sometimes babies cry, children pout, adults argue. Sometimes there's an empty chair at the dinner table, a subtle reminder of death or divorce. But if we care enough about this collection of kin, such things can be overcome. And if we look hard enough, we can see the calm amid the confusion. Far removed from the storm of sugar-fueled children, your mother is quietly reading a grandchild a bedtime story.

And so we return to our roots. If we can't, we call. But it's never the same. It's not the same as smelling bayberry and fiberglass, that holiday blend known only to families whose fathers build sailboats in the garage. And it's not the same as shooting a few baskets on the hoop that once seemed so tall.

To return means experiencing that strange feeling of being both visitor and resident, as if we are absentee owners holding titles to the property of the past.

On the one hand, we know this place will never again be home. On the other, we know it always will be home.

Miss Sofie

WHEN MY OLDEST SON, RYAN, was nine, Sally and I found ourselves worrying about which fourth-grade teacher he was going to get. Ryan could explain a zone defense and tell you most of the Seattle Mariners' batting averages, but he wasn't headed for anybody's All-American academic team. And looming in front of him was a teacher reputed to be a drill sergeant in a dress.

Her name was Miss Sofie. Upper 40s. Never married. And known to give homework as if Ryan's elementary school were Harvard Law.

"Let's put it this way," said one father, whose son had had Miss Sofie the previous year. "She gave a geography quiz on the last day of school."

Gulp.

My wife and I contacted the school's principal and requested that Ryan not be placed in Miss Sofie's class. He wasn't. We were relieved.

But a few days into school, the class Ryan was in was deemed too large; some students would have to be shifted to Miss Sofie's class. Ryan was among them. We were petrified.

On the day I walked Ryan into Miss Sofie's class, I felt as if I were Abraham taking Isaac up the mountain to the sacrificial altar.

Ryan didn't say much for a few weeks. Then one evening, as we finished dinner, he abruptly took his plate to the kitchen.

"Time to hit the books," he said.

Sally's eyes widened. I nearly spit out my milk. But as the school year unfolded, an amazing thing happened: Ryan fell in love with learning.

In the months to come, Ryan learned the locations and spellings of countries and cities he'd never heard of. He learned to organize his time, do homework, do research. He learned to count to ten in Norwegian. Recite poetry. Spell. Write. Weave. And figure the Mariners' batting averages without using a pocket calculator.

Above all, Ryan learned to be more responsible. Because he was being taught by a woman who understood the importance of responsibility. He learned to live more purposefully because he was being taught by a woman with great purpose.

As the school year wound to a close, Miss Sofie began missing classes here and there.

"She's sick," Ryan said.

Later, she missed a week.

The news ultimately hit like glass shattering: Cancer. But knowing Miss Sofie's feistiness—this was a woman who played the accordion and once lived on an Israeli kibbutz—we figured she would be back in the saddle come September, inspiring a new class of kids to memorize Carl Sandburg's *Fog* and to find Mozambique on a map.

But she never did come back. She died in July.

"You don't replace a Sherrie Sofie," a minister said at her service. "God threw away the mold."

"I don't think I'll ever have a better teacher," Ryan told me after hearing the news.

Not everybody was as fond of Miss Sofie. Some found her too rigid, too demanding, too domineering. But they were the exceptions, not the rule. "Miss Sofie's class was the last place I learned any geography," said one ex-student. "I had lots of good elementary teachers, but she stands out."

At the memorial service, many echoed such sentiments. "She was pretty much a traditionalist," said a fellow teacher.

After recess, girls in Miss Sofie's class entered the room first. If the flag salute wasn't done well, it was done over again.

After the flag salute, the class would sing a patriotic song—
The Star-Spangled Banner perhaps or *America the Beautiful*.
Each day, the class ran at least two laps around the field.

She believed in music, memorization, and manners. She
was a stickler for good grammar. She abhorred students saying
yep, nope, and *um*. If a child used too many *ums,* Miss Sofie
would politely remind him, "We don't speak *ummish* here. We
speak English."

When the class went to the library, Miss Sofie ranked its
behavior on a 1-to-10 scale. "Six and seven were satisfactory,"
Ryan said, "but Miss Sofie wanted eight, nine, or ten."

For Miss Sofie, wrong was wrong and right was right. She
was like the basketball coach in *Hoosiers,* who demanded the
ball be passed so many times before a shot was taken; he knew
it might look senseless to others, but it would breed what the
team needed most: teamwork and discipline.

"Her philosophy was, 'You only get what you expect,'" a
fellow teacher said. "She did not adhere to 'I-can't-do-it' philosophy, and she showed children they *could* do it."

Above all, she had a deep sense of purpose, a sense that her job
was not simply to fill all these little brains with facts, but to make
her pupils better, wiser, more well-informed, caring human
beings. To teach them to believe in themselves. To encourage
them to be more than they were, which is what good relationships do, be they husband-wife, parent-child, or teacher-student.

"She believed in me," said Ryan.

She would often remind her class that learning wasn't
easy—and I suppose that's true whether the subject is math or
geography or life or death. But because of her, a nine-year-old
boy whose favorite book was *Seattle Mariners Facts and Stats*
began reading *The Secret Garden*. And the boy's father learned
something about judging people without even knowing them.

Nearly a decade later, Ryan was faced with a huge challenge—convincing a college that, despite a good-but-not-great

3.3 GPA, he deserved to attend the school. His essay topic had to be on his most influential educational experience. He didn't hesitate writing about the obvious choice: Miss Sofie.

He was accepted to the school and, Lord willing, will graduate from it a few months from now—with a GPA higher than his high school mark.

And so, though she's gone, we see this woman's influence, like wind rustling through a wheat field. And we hold fast to our memories of a woman whose unforgettableness lies beyond her style and standards, in one simple thing: She cared about making children better than they were.

I'll remember Miss Sofie on the day Sally and I showed up early for a parent-teacher conference. We found her alone in the classroom, playing *Bicycle Built for Two* on the piano—with Carnegie Hall passion.

Now she is gone. But for anyone who's ever had a Miss Sofie in their life, the song goes on.

Fruits of Simplicity

IN 1994, TOM PENIX WAS HIRED as a graphics artist at the newspaper where I work. I found him to be one of the most talented, team-oriented people I've worked with in my 25 years in the newspaper business. He blended hard work with a wacky sense of humor that came through in all sorts of strange ways—like the time I took him to a college football game and he thanked me with an artsy trophy whose main ingredient was a mouth guard he'd found on the field after the game.

But though he seemed happy with life, I wondered. He and his wife, Elaine, had moved to Oregon from southern California, where Tom had worked for the *Los Angeles Times*. They already had two kids, were expecting a third, and two years later had a set of twins: seven people, ultimately, in a 1,450-square-foot house.

The family lived on Tom's paycheck. Kids were forever getting sick. Cars were forever breaking down. Plans for short vacations were forever getting put on hold—or scrapped altogether.

Amidst it all, however, I realized something one day: Tom Penix was among the most content people I'd ever met. And the reason, I discovered, was that, unlike so many people these days, he's built his life on the deeper things that money can't buy and circumstances can't provide.

"Long ago, before Elaine and I even had children, I had this dream—a literal dream—of seeing all these kids playing out in a field," Tom says. "They were my kids. Then one day, not long ago, I was out mowing the lawn and I stopped and looked out in this field and there were these kids—my *actual* kids—and I remember thinking: The Lord has given us what we asked for. I just felt so *rich*."

The Penixes' life is interwoven with simplicity and faith. And as I've come to know them, I've been reminded how often the truly content people fit none of the descriptions that we associate with the so-called "good life"—sprawling houses and expensive clothes and trips to exotic places.

Sometimes, the person living in a million-dollar home is the same person popping pills to dull the pain of living. And sometimes the person living in a 1,450-square-foot home is talking about feeling rich.

"Deprived? I actually feel privileged to have the life I have," says Tom. "I think of this one picture we have of Phoebe—she's our 6-year-old—smelling this big, ripe tomato and it's one of those moments you just can't buy with a ticket."

Tom, 42, and Elaine, 41, both have college degrees. And when they got married, both considered doing some foreign travel—perhaps with the Peace Corps or with a missionary organization. But when they started a family, they made some firm decisions.

First, that if at all possible, they would try to live on Tom's paycheck so Elaine could stay home with the children. It hasn't been easy, but they've done it. "I get to hear every funny thing my kids say as they grow up," says Elaine. "I have the satisfaction of knowing where they are all the time. Nobody takes care of them but me and Tom. And in the end, I won't be wondering if I could have done it better."

Second, that their home would become exactly that—the focal point for the family, not a fast-food restaurant where kids eat and leave, not an airport stopover, not a temporary place but a permanent place. When moving to Oregon, they bought a plain, three-bedroom rambler on one-and-a-quarter acres out in the country. It is not a house that's going to grace the pages of *Country Living*—four girls share one room—but there's enough room outside for kids to run and gardens to grow and tree forts to be built.

"One of our dreams was to have a yard where, if the kids were hungry, they could just pick something off a tree," says Tom. "And that's happening. There's lots of food in our backyard without much effort: cherry trees, blueberries....I just planted three pear trees. Eventually, I want this to be a place where, say, our grandkids could come from the city—a place that's unique and different."

And, third, that they wouldn't squander money on outside entertainment. The Penixes haven't been to a movie together in the last year. And they don't feel they've missed a thing.

"Our best date is, each morning, we fix a pot of coffee and either sit in bed or in the living room and drink coffee and just *talk*," says Tom. "Lately, the girls have wanted their own version of 'coffee' so they might join us and we'll look out the windows and see a bird or tractor and we always refer back to this street we lived on in southern California and say, 'Wouldn't see *that* on Lewis Avenue.' I feel like we're getting free entertainment. You look and see the sunflowers that are dying and so the birds come and take the seeds and then, later in the year, you see the birds digging up those seeds. We look out on a mint field and a filbert orchard and trees. Sometimes I'll stand at the kitchen window and think: *People pay money to get away from the city and be in a place like this.*"

Don't misread these folks. They aren't smug about their lifestyle choice, just confident in it. They shop at grocery stores, recently bought a new van, and take an occasional trip. But, for the most part, they have swum against the cultural current.

The family owns a used 19-inch TV set—no cable—but limits its use mainly to public broadcasting. "We don't want to use TV as a form of entertainment, not so much because it can fill the kids' minds with garbage but because we both feel it's such a waste of time," says Tom. "We want our kids to be more creative with their free time. We really push reading around here. And we're big on learning through experiences. I mean, we'll be outside explaining how intricately God designed a piece of fruit, how cool that is."

Sometimes, to give Elaine a break, Tom will load up the kids and take them for a drive in the country. "There are lots of farms out here so I'll show them emus and llamas and other animals. It's kind of a way of survival for Elaine, but it turns into a free zoo trip. The kids love it."

The family has one phone and no answering machine. Most of their vacation time is spent hanging out together as a family. They rarely eat out. "Occasionally, on a weekend, we might go to Burrito Boy but that's about it," says Tom. "Some people think we're depriving our kids but I think we're teaching them to appreciate things. When they go out to eat at a nice restaurant with their grandparents, they *appreciate* it. I mean, they think Shari's is a five-star restaurant."

Their children—Maggie, 14; David, 12; Phoebe, 6; and twins Sophie and Greta, 4—aren't being raised on packaged foods. Tom and Elaine make most of their meals, many of the ingredients from their garden or nearby farms.

There's a purpose to the plan: it not only saves money but it teaches the children that good things, like good meals, take time. "We're avoiding 'instant gratification,'" says Tom. "Day-to-day living takes time, hard work. You're going to raise empty kids if everything you do is 'instant.'

"One weekend each summer we'll pick fresh raspberries and fill up the back end of the van. We put them individually in plastic trays, then in freezer bags and we have them all winter long—you can't beat raspberry pancakes in January. We look at all this fruit around us and, really, to us it's like *gold*."

What's more, because so much of their food is "do-it-yourself," it frees the budget so they can give more to others. "When the Samaritan's Purse newsletter comes around, we have discussions with the kids about how blessed and rich we are in comparison to some others," says Elaine. "Many times a child has been willing to let go of a recent 'want' when he or she realizes that the money saved could feed a homeless child for a month or purchase a cow or goat for a family."

In the summer, Tom buys each of the kids a $4.99 membership in the junior club of Eugene's Class-A minor-league baseball team. "Ten games and a hat and a ball for $5," says Tom. "Plus, they get to run the bases after the game! They love it."

The children are taught to use their imaginations. Drama and music are big. When Tom and Elaine said no to toy microphones, the kids made their own—out of toilet paper tubes—and seem quite content with them, says Elaine.

"Our lives seem richer and less cluttered than those of many people we know," says Elaine. "If children are to grow up to be resourceful, creative, thankful, giving adults, they need to see real live examples while they are young."

The family makes good use of the public library and stays out of the malls. "The only time I'll go to the mall is if there's something specifically on sale that I know I need," says Elaine. "We don't go for the same reason you don't go strolling car lots unless you're going to buy—because you'll wind up wanting something you don't need."

Making choices like the Penixes make doesn't come without a cost. Tom, for example, has passed up some career-advancement opportunities. Recently, a Northwest metro paper made him a tantalizing offer; remember, this is a guy who once drew graphics for the *Los Angeles Times*. But after checking it out, Tom said no.

"It was sort of a dream job but I never had a peace about it," he says. "To live out in the country, I'd have had a one-hour commute. Lots of traffic. Higher prices. It just wasn't *us*."

So he turned it down, even though it went against the culturally accepted choice of opening the door whenever opportunity knocks. But that, say Elaine and Tom, is the first step toward more simple living: realizing you don't need to "go with the flow."

"I'm sure there are people who look at our lives and say 'boring,'" says Tom. "There are people who believe we have to have our kids in preschool to teach them how to be social. We think just the opposite. They're learning how to be social right here at home. Sure, they have friends over. They go to public schools. But we want to raise kids who are going to make a difference in the world.

"I guess our convictions are strong enough so we don't really care how the family down the street is raising their kids or if they think we're depriving our kids. We've been down that road and know there are better things in life than our mass culture promises."

Things like the recent scene in which 4-year-old Greta, mesmerized, stared at a flower. "All of a sudden she turns and says, 'Daddy, this is sooooo beautiful,'" says Tom. "I was thinking: This is what it's all about. She was expressing the same way I feel—such passion for a flower that God had created. It's moments like these that remind us how blessed we are."

PART IV

STRATEGY:

Charting Your Course

Without a chart, the skipper who is sailing into a stretch of water for the first time is virtually help-less, ignorant of exactly where his destination may be, of what might make a good port of refuge in a storm, of what the bottom is like, and of how close the bottom is to the top. With a chart, the sailor has a powerful ally and protector.

Fred Powledge, in *A Forgiving Wind*

It WAS A LATE-SUMMER SAIL, JUST SALLY AND I in my rookie sailing days. We'd decided to explore the far southwestern finger of Fern Ridge Lake and did so as a warm, early-evening wind blew steadily. It was a Friday night. We were in love. All was well.

Suddenly, *thud.*

We lurched forward in the cockpit. The fun drained from Sally's face. I mentally gulped.

"What was th—"

Thud.

Another lurch. The centerboard had hit something. Something firm. In my mind, panic pounded. Looking around, I realized we were way further south than I'd realized. That, coupled with late-season evaporation, meant only one thing: We were in water too shallow. Our centerboard, some five feet beneath the bottom of the boat, was ramming into underwater stumps.

I'd seen this stretch of the lake in winter, after the water had been lowered. It was sprinkled with the remains of trees, left from the days when they'd cleared forest land to put in this man-made lake. We were in trouble.

Thud.

The wind had picked up. Small swells were forcing us further south as I tried to bring us about and head us back toward where we'd come from. Finally, after a harrowing 15 minutes, we managed to get back into deeper water—our centerboard still somehow intact—and, shaken, sail safely back to safe waters.

A sailor needs to know not only where he is, where he's going, and why he needs to go there, but what's the best route to get there. Needs to know how to navigate the waters ahead. Needs to know how to avoid the danger areas.

Had I bothered to look at the charts stowed ten feet from where I was skippering the boat, I would have known this was an unsafe area. As it was, I'd assumed we were in deep waters. My problem was that I'd set sail with no particular strategy, and vision without strategy—or vision with *misguided* strategy—can be dangerous.

What Kind of Strategy?

"A simple man believes anything," says Proverbs 14:15, "but a prudent man gives thought to his steps."

Those who live with no particular strategy—no plan on how they're getting from point A to point B—are tossed and turned by the fickle winds of any capricious fad that blows their way. I find it fascinating to go to garage sales and see the various trends people have bought into—from exercise equipment to hobbies to self-help books, the personal equivalent of archaeological layers that have been exposed. But the very number of such pursuits that have come and gone suggests they don't seem to have satisfied.

People who simply "let life happen to them" rather than living it with intention are susceptible to flash-and-dash come-ons from marketers everywhere. Infomercials were made with precisely these folks in mind: diets that promise—no, absolutely *guarantee!*—overnight weight loss; investments that promise overnight gold mines; sand wedges that promise to "cut strokes off your game"—overnight, of course.

So, in our quest to transcend the pull of materialism, is the answer to live intentionally, to have a plan? Yes and no. It depends on the plan. Not all strategies will get you where you need to go.

A rookie sailor can, with the best of intentions, choose to sail directly into the wind. However, the laws of physics will laugh last; the only direction a sailboat cannot sail is dead into the wind. That sailor will fail not because he didn't plan or believe in his plan, but because he planned poorly. Not all strategies are equal.

A Mafia CEO might live a very intentional life, well planned, well carried out. But ultimately, it will not be fulfilling because the world is guided by God-ordained moral laws.

"How long, O men, will you turn my glory into shame?" says the Lord in Psalm 4:2. "How long will you love delusions and seek false gods?"

The veteran sailor can assume a similar cocksure attitude, subtly thumbing his nose at others and boldly seeking to go his own way, but he's doomed unless his strategy is sound. One evening, I was sailing slowly next to a group of racers and noticed that the crew of another boat seemed to be watching me with particular interest, as if somehow marveling at my skills. My ego puffed out like a Genoa jib. Then I realized I'd forgotten to unclip the boom from the back stay, which, in the world of sailing, is a little like sauntering coolly into a dinner party with one's zipper down.

It didn't matter whether I'd *assumed* I'd used good strategy; the fact is, with my boom unable to swing, my sail was going to catch only a smidgen of wind, and my boat was going nowhere fast. In this case, my mistake wasn't born of ego as much as oversight; but the fact is, my ignorance represented poor strategy.

What Kind of Change?

In the last decade, a sort of yuppified back-to-simplicity movement has sprouted here and there. From time to time, you read about people making huge lifestyle changes, giving up city life for rural life; trading the complexity of the corporate world for voluntary simplicity; unplugging themselves from technology to free themselves of the clutter in their lives.

A good thing? In many ways, yes. But in the face of materialism's pull, even those who outwardly appear to have fled from money, stripping themselves of wealth and belongings, may fall prey to a "simpler-than-thou" attitude, a sort of legalism where *what* we do becomes more important than *why* we do it.

In one book that I read about Americans who had given up the fast lane for the country lane, many of those profiled had become sort of well-heeled hermits. They were people whose new life had little to do with building stronger bonds with God and people and much to do with self-righteous escape. They were baby boomers— the "I'll get mine" generation, according to the late Chicago columnist Mike Royko—who'd left paths of broken relationships in their wake and were simply on their latest quest for self-fulfillment.

Indeed, unless it does an about-face, the wealthiest generation in U.S. history seems destined to leave a legacy of also being the most self-indulgent. If living the "simple life" is a valid strategy for living a more meaningful life, it must not become a selfish life where we simply run away from relationships and responsibilities. Our challenge is to live simply while not only keeping, but nurturing, the relationships that God says should be our priorities.

And it begins not with some grand plan to downscale—
though, again, that may be a valid choice of change—but deep
within our soul. The best strategy for bringing about change in
our lives—change that's morally based and built to last—
depends less on what we do on the outside than what we do on
the inside. Because what really guides our choices—what serves
as the centerboard for our life—is our heart. And that's what
God is concerned about most.

"Store up for yourselves treasures in heaven, where moth and
rust do not destroy, and where thieves do not break in and steal,"
says Jesus in Matthew 6:20-21. "For where your treasure is, there
your heart will be also."

I once interviewed a high-tech executive who unabashedly
believed that contentment was only a credit-card buy away. "I
thought I was having fun, taking exotic trips, buying Porsches
and jewelry," she told me. "But they were like drugs. The more
you did the more you needed it. You'd say, 'Last year I chartered a
55-foot boat so this year I'd better make it a 100-footer.' Money is
like Chinese food; you eat it and an hour later you're hungry."

Or as the author of Ecclesiastes put it: "Whoever loves money
never has money enough; whoever loves wealth is never satisfied
with his income" (5:10).

The woman's problem wasn't boats and cars and rings; her
problem was her heart. She wasn't sailing by the stars—fixing her
heart on the permanent things above—but sailing by peer pressure, the words of shrewd marketers, and a temporary world that
has taught us to feel empty and insignificant if we choose the
rowboat instead of the cruiser.

The Choice Makes All the Difference

So what's the right strategy? To sell all and become missionaries
on the garbage-strewn streets of Port-au-Prince, Haiti? Perhaps,
but not necessarily. The first step—simply put and complexly

lived out—is to seek the will of God; once you've made that connection, the necessary actions should follow.

And again, what's the will of God? That we pursue, grow, and sustain relationships with God and with people around us. If we focus on honestly doing God's will—not just going through the motions—the clutter of consumerism will loosen its grip on us, in the same way that weeds get choked out by the planting of a good ground cover.

Loosen its grip completely? No. As fallen people, we'll always be susceptible to greed; don't ever expect the howling winds of have-it-all-ism to stop blowing. But when setting sail, each of us makes a choice—conscious or not—whether we're going to sail by the stars or sail by ourselves; in essence, whether we will follow the supernatural Maker of those stars or the human creators of culture, that is, the world.

The choice makes all the difference. Writes J.I. Packer in *Hot Tub Religion:*

> Love of the world is egocentric, acquisitive, arrogant, ambitious, and absorbing, and leaves no place for any other kind of affection. Those who love the world serve and worship themselves every moment: it is their full-time job. And from this we see that anyone whose hopes are focused on gaining material pleasure, profit, and privilege is booked for a bereavement experience.

I read these words—particularly that "ambitious and absorbing" phrase—and can't help but think of a man who occasionally runs aground on such worldliness. That man is me.

And why do I run aground? Because from time to time, I love the world—and rely on my selfish ambition—more than I love and depend on the Creator of the world.

I think of an incident I told about in a previous book, *Where Roots Grow Deep,* but which begs retelling. How my wife had left on a short-term medical mission to the Dominican Republic and

I was looking forward to two weeks of immersing myself in a book project. And how I was to pick up my son from baseball practice, but he wasn't there. And how when I finally found him, unlike the father of the prodigal son who threw his wandering kid a party when he came home, I threw a fit.

Jason had walked to a friend's house, so I told him to stay put; I was coming to get him. My anger surged from head to foot and I was going 35 MPH in a twisting, 25-MPH neighborhood speed zone, when a handful of people crossing the street to a church wedding were suddenly in my headlights.

I slammed on my brakes and narrowly missed hitting them. Then I drove around the corner, pulled to the side of the street, and wept. I wasn't only grieved that I'd nearly killed four people; I was ashamed that, in my compulsive ways, I'd let my life drift so far from where it needed to be.

Packer was right; misplaced priorities can lead to a "bereavement experience." I'd been angry at Jason because his not letting me know where he was had cost me valuable time on *my* writing project. My own ambition, my own arrogance, had blinded me to what was really important—relationships, in this case, a link with a teenage son whom I'd shoved to the back shelf as I concentrated on me and only me.

My heart had hardened to the things that mattered. And life change must begin with the heart—it is, we're told, substance in a world of style. "These people," Jesus says of the Pharisees in Matthew 6:15, "honor me with their lips, but their hearts are far from me."

Change Begins with Trust

This poses the question: What kind of hearts should we have? Jesus answered the question with a reply that surprised His prideful disciples. You should, He said, have hearts of children. "Let the little children come to me," Jesus told the disciples, who had rebuked the little kids who had been brought to touch him.

"Do not hinder them, for the kingdom of God belongs to such as these. I tell you the truth, anyone who will not receive the kingdom of God like a little child will never enter it"

—Mark 10:14-15

Why hearts of children? Because children recognize their needs, their dependence. Children feel their vulnerability and react to it; adults mask their pain with everything from alcohol to acquisition, and try to pretend the pain isn't there.

Why hearts of children? Because children live simple lives. They do not adorn themselves with job titles and status symbols and ambitious agendas; they simply *are*. A friend of mine recently spent Christmas with his 10-month-old grandson, who joyously played in crumpled wrapping paper, unconcerned with whatever was in the box. I wonder if, as adults, we're too concerned with what's in the box—about what we're *getting* in life—to be able to experience such unbridled joy.

Why hearts of children? Because children are malleable. As adults, we stubbornly stay the course, no matter how bad the storm; pride can be a ruinous rudder in our lives. In the movie version of Sebastian Junger's *The Perfect Storm*, a sailboat flails about in a hurricane while two crew members plead with the captain to turn around and head for safer waters. He won't have it—not so much because he believes staying the course will lead to safety, but because his pride has blinded him from the truth.

But children, whether they know it or not at the time, are open to change—and make such change because of trust they put in someone beyond themselves.

I believe we're each born with a longing to connect with the One who created us. Too often, though, we try to fill that longing with something else. Though that "something else" can temporarily fill us, we'll ultimately realize—as did the woman who told me that her materialistic binges were like eating Chinese food—that we're still hungry.

"I am the bread of life," declared Jesus in John 6:35. "He who comes to me will never go hungry, and he who believes in me will never be thirsty."

Because we rely so much on the material, it's difficult for many of us to accept that the missing piece in life's puzzle could be spiritual: not something we can see, touch, buy, exchange, and get an upgrade on—but something far more mysterious, something that influences us unseen, like the wind.

Writes Deborah DeFord in *Seeking a Simpler Spirit:* "We struggle with the very idea of connecting with God because we're so used to focusing on the material part of life; we're comfortable with what we can quantify and prove."

Where Change Begins

God is beyond quantifying and proving. Unlike a VCR or computer or stereo system, He can't be programmed. He simply *is*. Do you see the irony? We try to squeeze God through our finite filters of materialism—so what's His net worth?—instead of understanding that He transcends our trivial pursuits. In the same way, even if we've chosen to live more meaningful lives, our first inclination is to tamper with the material, not the spiritual; the packaging—our outer lives—instead of the contents.

Yes, if we're intent on overcoming our materialistic lives, change should show up in the choices we make, in how we spend our time, money, and talents—in short, in what we treasure. But it must begin in a deeper place.

It's interesting that Jesus reserved most of His wrath for those who looked righteous on the outside but ignored the heart—those who lived for style, not substance. Speaking of the Pharisees, precursors of today's dress-for-success movement, He chided them because "everything they do is done for men to see" (Matthew 23:5).

Then as now, the Pharisees of the world deftly avoided getting to the core of what really mattered in life; instead, they assumed their weekly offering sanctified them in a special way. But Jesus said no.

> You give a tenth of your spices—mint, dill, and cummin. But you have neglected the more important matters of the law—justice, mercy and faithfulness....You clean the outside of the cup and dish, but inside they are full of greed and self-indulgence. Blind Pharisee! First, clean the inside of the cup and dish, and then the outside also will be clean (Matthew 23:23, 25-26).

Life change begins on the inside. "Blessed are the poor in spirit, for theirs is the kingdom of heaven" (Matthew 5:3). In other words, we're blessed not if we look invulnerable on the outside; we're blessed if we're genuinely vulnerable on the inside. Because out of that vulnerability comes an openness to "come about," to allow God to change us; out of that vulnerability comes the realization that, as Isaiah 64:8 says, "We are the clay, you are the potter."

In seeking a more meaningful life, you might choose to pull the plug on technology, slow down, and listen to life. Pick blackberries. Watch it snow—really *watch* it. Lie on the grass and look at clouds. Write a letter to a friend who expects one only at Christmas. Look closely at the words of a hymn. Thumb through a photo album. Notice the expression on your child's face as she draws. Write a poem.

But such actions begin much deeper: with humbling ourselves in childlike faith before Him; in what He knows, not what we know; in trusting that, just as nobody knows what's best for a boat like the people who made it, so does our Maker know what's best for those He made.

And those who choose to chart their own course, as I did when I let my too-busy life overshadow my son's?

Thud.

Haiti I: A Cup of Cold Water

IT IS EARLY EVENING. The woman has been in labor for days but the baby will not budge. The mother's pelvis is too small.

In most parts of the United States, a simple Caesarean section would be performed at a hospital, and everyone would live happily ever after. But this is not the United States.

This is Savane Carrée, Haiti, a remote mountain community with no hospital, no doctor, and no electricity. This is the most impoverished country in the Western Hemisphere, a place where living comes hard and dying comes far too easy. One in four children won't make it past age five.

For the American doctor, the choices are clear. If the woman is driven to a hospital in Dessalines, where he could safely perform a C-section, there is at least a chance. If not, the mother and baby will likely die. But separating Savane Carrée from the hospital are three hours worth of mud, potholes, and a river that must be crossed through—not over—seven times. At night.

Miss Maxine, a 59-year-old missionary, says the medical team has no choice. She hops behind the steering wheel and they're off. I watch as the Jeep, an IV fastened to its ceiling hand strap with twine, bounces down the road and vanishes into the darkness.

The scene is seared into my mind—like so many other scenes after I spent two weeks in this Third World country. I went to serve on a medical team from Washington state, coming home astounded at the needs in the world and amazed at the people willing to help meet those needs.

At 5 A.M., members of the Haiti Medical Team, sponsored by Yakima Free Methodist Church of Yakima, Washington, begin emerging from their gumdrop tents to begin a typical day. The Haitians, meanwhile, have already begun crowding to the front of the cinder-block church that will be converted into a clinic.

Most of the people have never seen a doctor and have walked or ridden donkeys miles to do so, winding their way on trails and roads from their thatch-roofed huts.

As word of the clinic spreads, the crowds begin arriving earlier and earlier each day. One night I hear some noises in the dirt-floor schoolhouse next to the church. Shining my flashlight inside, I see dozens of Haitians, wall to wall, waiting for morning and a chance to see a doctor or dentist.

During the two-week clinic, the team sees more than 2,000 patients. They dispense drugs, pull teeth, cleanse wounds, do minor surgery. They see it all: dehydrated children with only weeks to live. Tumors the size of tennis balls. Infected belly buttons caused by cutting the umbilical cord with a tin-can lid. Malnutrition. Worms. And more.

Amid such obstacles, team members wear buttons bearing the team motto: "No problem." The message? With God on our side, anything can be overcome—even a broken generator and a team-record ten flat tires.

Improvisation and duct tape help us survive. The side of a cardboard box becomes a splint. A chalkboard is turned over to become a pharmacy table. A plastic tarp is hung in the corner of the church to create an intensive care unit. We even improvise with our skills: A software engineer assists a dentist. A patent attorney fixes a major leak in Savane Carrée's water line. A homemaker helps an elderly woman take a pill. A college student scrubs a child's diseased skin.

One night, a sudden rain shower forces the team into the church to eat dinner. The worship service will begin in half an hour, and a few dozen Haitians have already arrived, seated on wooden benches. They quietly watch us eat as we try to ignore the unavoidable clash of haves and have-nots. Finally, the team begins sharing its food and cups of fruit drinks.

The Haitians, mostly children, gracefully accept. It is the gospel at its grassroots best—Matthew 10:42 with a raspberry twist.

"And if anyone gives a cup of cold water to one of these little ones because he is my disciple, I tell you the truth, he will certainly not lose his reward."

Quiet heroics abound. Once, just before a church service is to begin, a Haitian woman in the congregation begins hemorrhaging. With the help of a nurse, a doctor calmly takes the woman into the "ICU"—a corner of the church with a shower screen stretched in front of it—and stops the bleeding, then returns to sing Haitian praise hymns.

No problem.

As clinic continues, the doctors do what they can. Sometimes, nothing can be done. Working in the pharmacy one day, I'm handed a prescription card from a nurse. It prescribes only one thing: "Prayer."

Other times, the doctors save a life that probably would have been lost. A year before our team arrived, a boy was brought to the clinic with severe burns from a fire that was lit to ward off evil spirits. The previous medical team had treated him and rushed him to a hospital. Now he's back to visit—and he's healthy.

Three years earlier, tiny "Wizzy" was brought to the clinic on the verge of starvation. She was 19 months old and weighed only eight pounds—"a sack of bones," according to one doctor. Now, she's healthy, strong, and beautiful. Her mother shows up at the clinic with a basket of fresh eggs to say thank-you.

As our stay nears its end, the crowds grow larger. People try to bribe the guards with what little money they have. They pass babies through the iron bars to friends inside. So many push against the gates that the hinges on the iron door break—not because the crowd is unruly but because of its collective force.

It's hard to feel angry toward them; they only want to live, to overcome the pain that's gone on so long—like the Haitian woman in labor who left in the Jeep, her hand clutching the hand of a U.S. nurse who had voluntarily been with her since early that morning.

A week earlier, the nurse had been living safely in a cocoon of American comfort, a place where some see hardship as not being able to find where they left the TV remote. Now, as the Jeep bounces toward Dessalines, she holds the Haitian woman's hand and wipes the sweat from the woman's face as if the two were sisters. Black and white, rich and poor, young and old—the differences between the two women fade as the darkness deepens.

Miss Maxine, the missionary driving the Jeep, makes the usual three-hour trip to the hospital in a little more than two. The doctor works fast; at midnight—minutes away—the generator will kick off and he'll have to do the C-section by flashlight. He performs the surgery in 11 minutes.

In the sticky warmth of the Haitian night, a cry of hope interrupts, if only for a moment, this country's day-to-day despair.

It's a boy.

Haiti II: Seeing with New Eyes

Now comes the sorting out. The processing. The questioning. The contrasting.

One day, you're guarding a door at a makeshift medical clinic in the mountains of Haiti, trying to stand stoic while a mother lifts her child to you. You don't have to know Creole to understand what she's saying; her eyes transcend the language barrier. *Please, take my baby and make her better.*

Two days later, you're sitting in seat 21A, heading back to America. "Can I get you a pillow?" asks the flight attendant. "Something to drink?"

It's hard to avoid the cultural bends when you return from two weeks in the most impoverished country in the Western Hemisphere, particularly when you return to the most affluent country in the world.

You leave America thinking the world is one way. You return realizing it's not. And no matter how many *National Geographic* pictures you've seen, being there is different. Seeing the outstretched arms of beggars, hearing the pounding of voodoo drums, touching the hand of a sick child—it's different. It's *real*. And I'm different because I experienced it.

You come back feeling as if you've witnessed a crime. On the one hand, you want to forget what you've seen; that way, you won't feel obligated to get further involved, won't feel uncomfortable, won't feel a threat to your personal American Dream. On the other hand, you know you can never forget.

You can never forget those eyes. The chiseled faces of those waiting behind the iron-bar door, hoping you'll let them in before the clinic closes. The teenage boy who held his little brother's hand as he led the little boy through the clinic—such trust in the little tyke's big brown eyes. The father who held his dehydrated child in his arms all day long, giving him occasional sips of water as the doctor had requested.

As team photographer, should I take a picture? The father nodded that it was all right. As I started to focus, the father tried to prop up the listless child to make him look healthier and happier than he was. I couldn't click the shutter. Instead, I stammered an apology in broken Creole and walked outside for fresh air.

Now, I can't seem to shake the scenes. I find myself mentally contrasting life in Haiti to life in America. Because a trip to Haiti does more than afford a glimpse at another culture. It forces you to examine your own.

Often the tides of here and there meet with riptide fury. One day you're seeing Edwin—a Haitian boy the same age as your oldest son—point to his stomach to signify he's hungry. The next day you're standing in a supermarket line, seeing the cover of *Self* magazine: *Money hungry?* teases a headline. *Too much is not enough.*

A few days after I returned, I was at the newspaper office where I worked, writing about my Haiti experience. I had just finished a sentence about people who live in cardboard boxes in Port-au-Prince when the phone rang. The caller said he had a problem that might make good column fodder: He was trying to buy a 55-foot, $300,000 yacht and believed he was being "ripped off" by the seller.

As nicely as I could, I told the man he didn't have a problem. Two weeks in Haiti makes you redefine your idea of trouble. You see, more clearly than ever, America's thirst for material things. And how much we take for granted.

Mike Buehler, a Yakima, Washington, dentist on the team, had treated a Haitian man the year before our team went and had given him a return-visit card. A year later, there was the man, patiently clutching the soiled card. "Yet some of my patients at home come unglued if we're running 10 minutes late," he said.

Wayne Schneider, the team's pastor, was awed at the enthusiasm of the Haitians who came to sing hymns of joy each evening in the church. If anyone had reason to give up on God, it would seem to be people mired in pain and poverty.

"It's going to be hard," said Schneider, "going home and hearing parishioners complain that they don't like the looks of the church bulletin."

Pain and suffering, I realize, are equal-opportunity human conditions; you'll find them in the cushiness of an American hospital and in a cinder-block clinic in Haiti. But here, they come in scattered raindrops; there, in incessant showers.

Just like the Haitians, we Americans are products of our history, our environment, our experiences. As such, we needn't wallow in guilt because we've been blessed with clean water, modern hospitals, and food aplenty. But neither should we save our appreciation for the 30-second prayer before we dig into our Thanksgiving turkey.

Neither should we wear materialistic blinders to protect us from Third World realities.

And neither should we backhandedly rationalize that the need is too great for us to help.

Watching the throng of Haitians unable to get into the clinic each day, we found it easy to start wondering whether any of us could really make a difference, whether what we were doing really mattered.

One night, team members met to spill some emotions about what we were experiencing. There, the story was told of a boy who was walking along a beach, throwing objects into the ocean.

"What are you doing?" an old man asked.

"These starfish have washed ashore and if they don't get back in the water they'll die," said the boy.

Pointing to thousands of starfish lying stranded, the man said, "You'll never be able to save them all, so what does it matter?"

The boy looked down at the starfish in his hand.

"Well, sir," he said. "It matters to this one."

A League of His Own

AS A NEWSPAPER FEATURES WRITER in the early '80s, I had just finished interviewing an author who was on a national book tour—when I couldn't resist.

"I wonder if you'd mind autographing a copy of your book for my brother-in-law," I said. "He stands for everything you've written about."

Sitting across from me in a plush Seattle hotel, Joseph L. Troise didn't hesitate. He reached into his briefcase, pulled out a copy of his book, and autographed one to Dr. Glenn Petersen.

Its title? *Dare to Be Dull.*

In a world of trendiness, my brother-in-law Glenn lives in a league of his own. Nobody I know is so hopelessly out of it. Some of my colleagues at work believe *I* fit that category, that I live this Ward Cleaver life of perpetual unexcitement. But when the subject comes up, I tell them I pale in comparison with Dr. Glenn Petersen—or as I call him, "Dr. Dull."

He is to flamboyance what Shaq O'Neal is to hair.

His idea of living on the edge is drinking non-diet pop. One Christmas, I gave him the "Glenn Petersen 12-Month-a-Year Sleep Calendar," each month featuring a photograph of him having fallen asleep at some family function: August, for example, showed him lying on the beach, and December, snoozing in front of a Christmas tree.

He is, if I'm not mistaken, the last U.S. citizen to not have an answering machine, having only recently made the switch from rotary-dial. He could name two Beatles, maybe three. He is a hopeless romantic, having once bought his wife, Ann, a

Pyrex bowl for Valentine's Day. *(Promise her anything, but give her Pyrex.)* At Christmas, he traditionally gives her a beef stick.

Ironically, my first memory of Glenn Petersen is perhaps my most exciting memory of him. We were college students on a backpack trip in Oregon's Eagle Creek Wilderness Area and had stopped at a small stream for a breather when one of us—probably me since Glenn would never do anything this exciting—splashed the other.

Watching this incident were our girlfriends—two sisters, meaning that though Glenn would soon grow out of such youthful excitement, he was secretly as intent as I was on impressing his love interest. (Wait—*love interest* is an overexciting term. His *friend.*) Thus did the incident lead to a full-blown wrestling match between the two of us—in the middle of this creek.

Other than sparring on a few political issues, golf, and Scrabble, we've never tangled since. Glenn's getting excited about something would be like a hemophiliac's getting a scratch; it could be dangerous.

We each grew up—well, sort of—and married one of those sisters, though right up to the time of his wedding, Glenn insisted he and Ann were "just good friends."

Now 48, he's been married 24 years and has three teenage daughters, none nearly as dull as he. In those 24 years, he has bought one house, four cars (only one that was new), and a two-burner outdoor barbecue that, for him, was the materialistic equivalent of buying a $50,000 Humvee.

When his 1984 Chevrolet Suburban broke down a few years ago, he had a new engine put in rather than buy another vehicle. Two days later, that engine died. He had a third engine put in it.

"He has that Lutheran thriftiness," his cousin told me the other day.

He is a doctor—a family practitioner—who lives on a quiet, nondescript street in a small, semi-dull town. Each weekday morning he walks five blocks to his office, which is one block from the hospital. He often takes his own lunch, the highlight of which is Ritz crackers.

At home, you drop in on him and he'll either be asleep on the couch or engrossed in a magazine such as—no, I'm not making this up—the *American Journal of Gastroenterology*.

Once, he was forced to attend a medical convention in Hawaii. "I don't *get* that place," he said upon returning, glad to be home after what he described as a week of too many people and too high prices. (He didn't mention anything about sun, sand, and surf.)

Nor does he *get* eating out, which is fine with me, since it's embarrassing to be sitting in a plush restaurant and have him ask the tuxedoed waiter if his entree can be "biggie-sized." Once when his family was visiting us outside of Seattle, Sally, Ann, and I talked of going into the city for dinner. "You mean you want to drive all the way to Seattle [20 minutes away] just to *eat?*" he said.

He is, to my knowledge, the only person ever to complete a triathalon using a bicycle that had a kid's seat on back.

Prestige has never meant a thing to Glenn; when his three daughters got out of their baby stage and the family needed more room, the family didn't buy a $750,000 hillside home; they remodeled the basement to make a room that two of the girls would share.

For 23 years, Glenn and I and two other friends have gathered for a yearly golf tournament. In that time, two of the golfers in the group have combined to buy probably 10 sets of golf clubs. I've gone through two sets. Glenn has bought one new set of irons (early '80s) and a few new woods.

Until recently, he would show up on the first tee in what we called "The Little Red Riding Hood" sweatshirt, a fine choice if, say, you're changing the oil in your car or want to look like a Peanuts character, but hardly the fabric of choice for a nice golf course. After taking literally two decades of razzing about the sweatshirt, Glenn broke down a few years ago—and bought a new red sweatshirt (though he still occasionally wears the old one).

In the early years, Glenn got less excited about the golf part of the tournament than about finding empty pop and beer cans in the rough along the course. He'd stuff them in his bag. He would show up at the eighteenth hole smelling of stale beer, smiling broadly, knowing he had, like, $1.35 in returnable cans.

"Glenn," I'd remind him, "you're a *doctor.*"

He's never let that kind of stuff go to his head. He has the unassuming presence of a barn swallow. In fact, Glenn once went golfing with me and a work pal of mine, and toward the end of the round, my colleague asked me what Glenn did for a living.

"He's a doctor," I said.

"Yeah, *right,*" said the guy.

☾   ☾   ☾

HAITI CHANGED EVERYTHING. Haiti not only splashed water in my face about my own materialistic ways, but made me see my brother-in-law in a whole new light. Made me understand him like never before.

Nearly every year for the past 15 years, Dr. Dull hops on an airplane and flies across the country to Miami, then on to Haiti, where he spends two weeks working in a medical clinic put on by Christians.

For years, he'd encouraged me to join him. Finally, I did. I was the jack-of-all-trades guy. I did everything from change tires to take photographs to serve as a guard, preventing people from sneaking into the clinic ahead of people who had been waiting in line for hours.

I remember exactly when I realized the character of the man whom I loved to make fun of—and who, to be honest, enjoyed being made fun of, at least most of the time.

It was at the end of a long day in the clinic, which we fashioned during the day inside a cinder-block church that was then used for evening worship each night. While I worked in the pharmacy dispensing pills, Dr. Dull and the medical staff had probably seen more than 200 patients.

Then came word: A *top top*, a Haitian bus that carries way more people—and animals—than it was designed for, had flipped. Half-a-dozen people had been injured, some seriously. From a distance, I watched as Glenn and the medical staff calmly stopped what they were doing and took care of the passengers who were brought into the clinic.

As I watched him tend to these people in need his hands covered in blood—I saw my brother-in-law more clearly than I'd ever seen him before. I appreciated him like never before. I think I saw the rest of the story, the story that was always there but that I'd never seen, at least not up close like this.

And I saw something an hour later that hammered it in all the deeper. The clinic had closed; nearly everyone was off to dinner, to unwind, to relax from what had been by far our most difficult day, to escape the emotional intensity of it all. For some reason, I wandered from our campsite back to the clinic. There, by himself, was my brother-in-law, quietly setting up the nickel-and-dime sound system for the evening church service.

In the years to come, Glenn would bring his wife and three daughters to Haiti for three months. They would go to Rwanda.

They would arrange for—and help pay for—Haitians with serious medical needs to fly all the way to their small, semi-dull town 4,000 miles away, and stay in the Petersens' home, sometimes for weeks, while waiting for and recovering from surgeries.

In America, most people believe that how much you earn is how much you should spend. They do not.

They gathered musical instruments from people within their church and had them sent to Haiti, so the people would have new and different ways to make joyful noises unto the Lord. Year after year they went back, setting up the medical clinic in the cinder block church.

Since the time I went to Haiti with Dr. Dull, I've never seen my brother-in-law in the same way again. Oh, I still make fun of him—there's even talk of a Glenn Petersen Sleep Calendar II—and I pester him about when he might join the twenty-first century and buy an answering machine. But deep inside I understand who he really is, beyond the comical persona I'd created for him and paraded at family gatherings.

Now, when I think of him walking to work, I think of him not as Dr. Dull or even Ward Cleaver, but simply as a man with so much purpose in his stride that he can't be concerned over whether he's keeping in step with the rest of the world.

Instead, he just walks to where he knows he needs to go.

Against All Odds

I MET HIM WHILE WALKING on a country road. He was about ten years younger than me, and riding a bicycle so swanky, it looked like it cost more than my car.

As a newspaper columnist, I was on the first day of a five-day, 45-mile walk to get a backpacker's-eye view of the community where I lived. I would write five columns after my journey to report what I'd found after a hike in and around suburbia.

The young man, about 25, was surprisingly open about his life. He had been married for two years, he said, but he and his wife were getting divorced. After some more conversation, I gently asked why. He didn't hesitate to tell me.

He gave me a long and twisting tale that basically boiled down to this: He loved to ride his bicycle long and far. She did not. The solution? Divorce.

We talked some more. He rode off his way; I walked off mine. But I couldn't help thinking about how much the world has changed in just a few generations. I couldn't help thinking about how different the pain threshold is today from what it was 50 years ago. I couldn't help thinking about Jim and Lou, a couple I'd interviewed not long before I met the bicyclist.

Fifty years before, on a warm day in Butler, Missouri, Jim and Lou handed a justice of the peace two bucks and vowed to love each other for better or for worse.

They got the worse.

Today, we married types complain about the hardship of juggling careers, kids, and Visa payments. It was never that simple for Jim and Lou, not when you start your marriage with $5, you're both teenagers, and neither one of you got past eleventh grade. Not when your first home is a dirt-floor tent, when you spend your honeymoon working at a sawmill, or when you go job-hunting on freight trains. Not when an accident puts your husband in a coma for a week, your son is born retarded, and, when you finally build your dream house, it has to be moved.

"We've come a long way from that five dollars," said Jim, a hint of Midwest farm drawl in his voice.

No, this couple didn't become wealthy, start a chain of successful franchises, or coauthor a bestselling book. They did help open the first school for the mentally retarded in the state of Washington. And they did become foster parents to a handful of children.

But perhaps the greatest accomplishment has been staying married—and in love—for half a century despite odds that would have sunk most marriages. They made a promise and kept it, an admirable deed, particularly in our age of broken promises.

When the couple started out, they didn't have access to marriage seminars, psychotherapists, or paperback how-tos. All they had was love, the Lord, and the will to stay together, regardless of what came their way.

And plenty came.

They met in 1936 at a church conference in Iowa, where Jim was raised. He was 19; Lou was 17. With the conference over, 300 miles separated the two. But Jim couldn't forget about the Missouri farm girl, so he hitchhiked to see her. After that visit, he scrounged up $50, bought a 1926 Chevrolet coupe, and proposed.

Five people showed up for the wedding, including Jim and Lou. Lou's father, not excited about losing a daughter he cherished, refused to come. But he gave the couple $5, which was all they had to start their married life.

At the time, the country was still in the throes of the Depression. An uncle gave Jim a job in his sawmill. Jim worked six days a week, made $14 a month, and was nearly killed when a steam engine exploded right in front of him.

Later, in Kansas City, Jim was riding down the street on a motorcycle. A car hit him from behind. He flew 25 feet in the air and skidded on the pavement for another 25 feet.

"My head went through the grille of a car's radiator," he remembers.

His landlord phoned Jim's mother in Iowa to report that her son was dead. He wasn't, of course. After a week in a coma, he regained consciousness.

In 1940, Jim and Lou were living in the basement of her folks' house in Nevada, Missouri, where Jim would walk five miles to his dollar-a-day service station job. One Saturday night, he came home from work, slumped in the chair and told Lou, "There's gotta be something better in the world."

The next morning, they packed their bags and began a four-month trip to Seattle, hitchhiking and hopping freight trains. Once, they were riding in the back of a watermelon truck that crashed. They survived. Another time, they were nearly beaten by club-wielding "railroad bulls," brawny men hired by the railroads to keep uninvited passengers off the freight trains. They survived.

From North Dakota to Spokane, Washington, they rode the rails; train whistles became a familiar sound. They made money by picking apples.

In Seattle, Jim got a job in a lumber mill, but he was laid off when World War II started. He found a job as a pipe fitter in a shipyard and, after four years, was able to afford the couple's lifelong dream—a home. Jim built it himself, painstakingly nailing every board in place. But before the house was finished, the state announced that a new freeway was going to be built right through their living room.

The house was moved. A few months later, as the two were finally enjoying the fruits of their labor, disaster struck: The house burned down. The local newspaper interviewed Jim at the time.

"Well, we started our married life in a tent," the article reported him as saying. "I guess we can do it again."

And, of course, they did. Soon, they were blessed with a son. He was born mentally retarded. But Jim and Lou didn't wring their hands and become recluses. Instead, they founded a school for children with disabilities, the first in the state.

"The Lord," said Jim, "has been good to us."

For years, the two kept busy putting on free square-dance parties in a small dance hall they added onto their house. Lou baked cookies. Jim did the calling.

On Sunday mornings, they drove disabled children to church in a van that Jim himself customized to accommodate wheelchairs.

They attribute their half-century of marriage to some simple things. "Learn to give and take," said Lou.

"Think of the other person," said Jim.

They celebrated their 50-year anniversary by renewing their vows at their church. And by remembering what they went through to get there.

Sometimes I think of that young man on the bicycle and wonder if it was worth it—if being able to ride a bicycle whenever he pleased was worth breaking a lifetime commitment to a woman he once vowed he'd love for a lifetime. And sometimes I think of Jim and Lou, and the lesson they taught me about perseverance in a world that can be cold.

And I worry about America.

"Every now and then we'll hear the whistle of a freight train," Jim told me. "We just look at each other and smile."

The Houdini Syndrome

ONE WEEK LAST SPRING, I WORKED my normal 40-hour week at the newspaper, gave three speeches, and helped organize and emcee a teachers' appreciation event at our church.

One day during that same week I arose at 3 A.M., drove four hours to Mount St. Helens in Washington state to gather information for a 20-years-after-the-volcanic-eruption column, drove four hours back home, and wrote the column while watching my son play a high school baseball game.

Having made my deadline, I arrived home at 9 P.M. and was greeted with the news from my wife that the plumber had said the 30-foot-long trench I had dug for a new water main needed to be another foot deeper—by 10 A.M. the next morning.

The next morning I got up, went to a 6 A.M. Point Man meeting, had breakfast with a young man in our church, dug the trench, and was at work by 10.

I am the poster boy for overcommitment. And I'm not particularly proud of that. We all have our weaknesses, and if I look at my life in the last decade, running too fast has been mine. Oh, I could justify that it's nearly all good stuff I run toward—I'm not the guy blowing two hours watching trash TV or playing two rounds of golf a week while my sons wonder why Dad never shows up for their games.

I could match my attendance at kids' games with nearly any parent and come out on top. I could rationalize that I've never had a nervous breakdown or resorted to any sort of illicit drugs—pop isn't illegal, is it?—to keep myself going.

Still, I have to face the reality that I'm far busier than I should be.

The good news is, I'm changing; the bad news is, that's like a 400-pound man saying he's going on a diet.

At times, my weeks have this Houdini quality about them: I bind myself in handcuffs and crawl into a trunk. The trunk is wrapped with chains. Then the trunk is dropped to the bottom of the East River to see if I can break free and swim to the surface without drowning.

Thus far, I've gotten out of the jam every time, broken the surface of the water just before my lungs are about to burst.

But though that might equate to success in the world's eyes, it does not in God's eyes. Because enslaving ourselves like that asks a price, though we're often so desperately trying to unshackle ourselves that we don't take the time to notice.

For me, that price has been a number of things:

A subtle, but real, loss of patience: When you're tired, anger more easily gains a foothold on you. It may not be a four-letter-word, dog-kicking, fist-slamming barrage of anger, but I know it's there. And I know it sometimes gets used against the people I love the most.

A subtle, but real, loss of creativity: When you're tired, you're more apt to settle for the ordinary when, somewhere deep inside, you might find the extraordinary.

A subtle, but real, loss of control over the more mundane aspects of life: checking accounts that need more consistent pruning, financial matters that need more plowing and planting, closets and dressers that need more consistent weeding.

A subtle, but real, loss of awareness of myself and the world around me: It's hard to stop and smell the roses when you can't even find the garden. It's hard to know how you might need to change if you never look in the mirror.

But the more serious price has come in the areas that I'm called to make my priorities: my relationship with God and my relationships with others, in particular my wife.

I've given time to both, but it hasn't been the quantity, or quality, they deserve. Again, I look good on paper: I'm an elder at our church, I teach Sunday school, I occasionally preach a sermon, I speak to men's groups. But I know, deep down, that God doesn't want a resume *from* me; He wants a relationship *with* me. And when you wedge God into your daily planner as if He were just another line on the To-Do List, that relationship suffers.

Likewise, I could point out trips I've taken with my wife, presents I've given her, dinners out we've shared. But I know, deep down, that she'd trade such things for more consistent "ordinary" time with me, time that might be nothing more than a walk around the block but which is given with my full attention, not as some sort of parenthetical phrase in the midst of a more significant sentence.

In terms of overcommitment, most people's problem is rooted in the workplace. I'm weird that way; that hasn't been my Achilles' heel. When I was 29, I shifted from covering sports to features, in part because my oldest son was 4 years old and I realized I was going to miss lots of his life if I had to work nights and weekends as sports requires.

I've known people who purposely worked through lunch or stayed late because they didn't want to *appear* as though they were slacking. When I was in my early 30s, I decided I didn't care what my colleagues thought; while still committed to working hard, I was going to go home for lunch and see my wife and kids when my work schedule made it practical. And I was going to come to the newsroom early—when nobody is there to witness your so-called dedication—and try not to stay late—when your so-called dedication is on full display.

I remember thinking:

The folks who win Pulitzer Prizes are the ones who stay longer.
You're making a conscious decision to not be as good as you could be.

You're sabotaging your chances to jump to a larger, metro newspaper.

My decision seemed to go against the very passion that drove me, but I made it and haven't regretted it in the least. With one son off to college and the other going soon, I look back on the time I spent with them and feel good about that decision. I wouldn't trade the extra time I spent at home for a dozen Pulitzers.

Because, you see, I've come to learn you *can't* have it all. So you have to decide what you want and what you're willing to give up. Some people decide what they want more than anything is to be successful in business and thus are willing to sacrifice their family to get there. I'm not among them.

But any chest-beating on my part that this might call out must be quelled by the realization that although I had my workplace life under control, the rest of my life was spinning out of control.

Part of my problem, I've realized, was a false notion I harbor that suggested, not only *could* I have it all, but I *must* have it all. Not in a materialistic sense; I've long since reconciled myself to the fact that I'm never going to be the guy who dies with the most toys—and frankly, I'm OK with that. But if not in the area of acquisition, until recently I've felt compelled to have it all in the area of outside-work accomplishments.

I've felt compelled to be some sort of Church Superman: It's not enough to be an elder—you must also teach Sunday school, volunteer for church cleanup, and emcee this event and that.

It's not enough to give my Kidsports baseball team year-end certificates; they must be *the best* year-end certificates, complete with color photos, statistics, and pithy quotes from the coach.

It's not enough to research a subject for a profile; you must know everything even remotely related to that person, including her entire genealogy.

If I'm starting to sound neurotic, it's only because I am—at least in packing eight days into a seven-day week. But again, I'm slowly changing. Slowly turning my too-busy life around in the same way a 700-foot cruise ship turns around—very slowly, but deliberately. When, by design or not, you've built momentum in one direction, it's hard for that momentum to be removed, much less go in another direction.

Sometimes it takes a wake-up call to get our attention. Ten years ago, in *More to Life Than Having It All,* I wrote of getting so blindly busy that I didn't take time to scrape the ice off my windshield one morning; rushing to a meeting, barely able to see out, I turned a corner and rammed my car up on a curb. It came to rest just in front of a telephone pole that would have creased the front left of the car like an aluminum can crinkled against a crowbar; who knows what it would have done to me.

Alas, wake-up calls wear off. While that incident momentarily got my attention, it obviously has worn off in the decade since. Then a less dramatic, but more insightful, wake-up call came my way.

Until recently, I headed a team of teenagers from our community who wrote, photographed, and illustrated a section of the newspaper each week. Over the months I got to know and care about these young people. So I was devastated when Mario, one of our students—one of my favorites—was killed in an automobile accident.

But things involving his death had to be done—and the rest of my world couldn't stop while I helped. I needed to help the other students deal with this loss. I needed to answer the TV reporters' questions. I needed to lobby my publisher for a scholarship to be offered in Mario's name. I wrote a column for the paper about him. I spoke at two memorial services. I remember thinking: *Just make it until Saturday. You have nothing planned. You can rest and recharge.*

Finally, Saturday came. I was completely drained. I headed off on my traditional Saturday-morning run. Then, midway through my four-mile course, it dawned on me: I had signed up to help spruce up the church that morning.

I was tired. I was angry. But I knew what must be done: I turned around and headed home. I *had* to be at that church.

"The church will get cleaned up without you," said Sally, knowing my emotional state.

She didn't understand. I peeled off my clothes, took a shower, and got on my work clothes.

"I signed up," I said. "I told Dave I'd be there."

"You need to rest."

"I made a *promise*," I said.

"Dave will understand."

"No, *you* don't understand!"

I hurled the words at her with intent to hurt. And I could see the pain in her face. Suddenly, the scales fell off my eyes and I saw the madman I'd become. Mario's death, years of overcommitment, physical exhaustion—all converged into this moment of introspection.

I held Sally—she held me—and I wept. Out of exhaustion. Out of shame. But, more than anything, out of necessity. For I desperately needed to take stock of my compulsion to run so hard, to lose perspective, to gradually fall into thinking that, without me, the world would somehow stop revolving.

I believe we're called to give our best to God; our work should be done with gusto and quality. But we're also called to lives of balance, and when we get out of balance, our work becomes a legalistic going-through-the-motions, not something filled with heart. Our work becomes more important than the people who it's intended for. Our lives are guided by our heads and not our hearts.

But as I said, slowly I'm changing. I no longer let guilt goad me into saying yes whenever someone calls and asks if I can speak. Though honored to be considered, I no longer believe, just because someone else thinks I'm the right person to write a book or an article, that I actually am. I no longer believe I have to have a hand in everything at church.

I have a strategy, nothing deep or involved, but a starting place. I'm starting to block off time each week for Sally and me. In spring and summer, I'm scheduling solo sails for myself at Fern Ridge Lake, where I can think and pray and relax and simply *be*. I'm trying to discipline myself to reach for the word of God, not the newspaper, first thing each day.

Slowly, my ship is turning. I think of the story of Mary and Martha, how Jesus was coming to visit and they reacted so differently from each other. Mary sat at His feet, listening. Martha was distracted by all the preparations that had to be made—and by the fact that Mary wasn't pulling her weight with the work.

"Martha, Martha," said Jesus. "You are worried and upset about many things, but only one thing is needed. Mary has chosen what is better" (Luke 10:38-41).

At times, I relate to Mary: Generally speaking, I believe I've focused my life on the right things. But at times, I'm a Martha. I can be writing books, giving speeches, teaching classes—and yet still be so distracted that I miss what really matters: my relationship with God and with those around me.

The world does not need more Marthas, more Houdinis, more poster boys for overcommitment. The world needs more Marys, people who focus on what—and who—is important.

On that Saturday morning I'd signed up to help clean, the church got spruced up just fine without me. Dave understood. The world kept spinning. And thanks to a wife who cared enough to question my compulsiveness, I'm struggling to turn this ship around.

Which is good. It only takes a Houdini one failed escape attempt to end an otherwise promising life.

Caught in the Cross Fire

"ALL RISE."

The gavel falls, the judge sits down, the trial begins. Six years before, in a church, the couple had said "I do" to each other. Now, in the stark coldness of a courtroom, they begin the painful process of saying "I don't."

Sitting within 15 feet of each other, the man and woman avoid eye contact at all costs. Though legally still married, they have become petitioner and respondent, not husband and wife; enemies, not allies. The connection between them is as lifeless as the bricks on the courtroom walls.

"Just think," says a courtroom reporter between sessions. "They once called each other sweetheart."

We've all watched a marriage begin, but few of us have watched a marriage end. From the back row of the courtroom, I've come to watch such an ending, to witness one of the divorce wars fought in thousands of courtrooms across America each day.

Once, I assume, these two people had visions for a happy future. But their strategy for making that vision come true has somehow failed miserably.

It isn't pretty, this scene. But then, to understand the importance of wearing a seat belt, sometimes you need to look at a mangled car.

The man and woman, whom I chose at random, are your typical middle-class family. They're nice-looking and dress well. They're not part of a dysfunctional family, a counselor has ruled. They're simply a couple who decided to split up because of "irreconcilable differences."

A judge will decide who will get everything, from their cars to their Funk & Wagnall encyclopedias. But the big question is who will get custody of their three-year-old son.

As the trial unfolds, a chasm of contrasts separates then and now, wedding and dissolution. The two are flanked not by a best man and a maid of honor bearing rings that will unite, but by attorneys armed with evidence that will divide.

There is no photographer capturing each priceless memory, only a court reporter recording each verbal volley.

There is no triumphant music, only the tinny sound of testimony spoken into microphones.

There is no festive throng of family and friends, only empty benches and a handful of supporters waiting in the lobby.

Between sessions, the two gather with their friends and families in the lobby, like boxers going to their respective corners.

The woman's attorney argues that the man is an irresponsible parent, as shown by the raising of his 12- and 14-year-old sons—his by a previous marriage—who lived with the couple. He doesn't believe in structure and discipline. He doesn't care if the kids do their homework. The woman, the attorney says, has cared enough to set boundaries, build structure, and require accountability.

The man's attorney counterattacks. He argues that the woman has been abusive to the children. She has hit them, screamed at them, locked them out of the house in their underwear. The man, he says, has cared enough to help the boys with their homework, calmly handle friction, and cook an abundance of meals, particularly pancake breakfasts.

On topics ranging from pearl necklaces to dented trucks, from flunked classes to stapled cats, the attorneys continue their assaults, dropping smart bombs to do damage in strategic positions. Pierced ears, paddles, and broken pickle jars—these are among the subjects that come into play in deciding which parent would be best for a little boy who has no say in the matter.

At one point, the woman is on the witness stand. "You talk about a time when [your husband] put you into a bedroom," says her husband's attorney.

"He *threw* me into the bedroom, yes."

"Do you remember why you were placed in the bedroom by him?"

"He was angry at me."

"Do you know why?"

"No."

"Wasn't it because he had just separated you from having a fight with one of the older children?"

"No."

Minute by minute, hour by hour, day by day, the evidence grows like a gnarled juniper tree. The judge hears about the time the three-year-old was slapped for pushing the VCR buttons during *The Little Mermaid*. The time he cried when being shifted from one parent to another. And the time he was allowed to ride in the back of a pickup truck.

What's true? What's not? Amid this family's chaos, it's difficult to tell. While the battle continues, the propaganda war heats up, each side describing incidents in vastly different ways.

For a few days, the two older boys' neighborhood friends—ranging from age 9 to 14—come to testify. They gather excitedly in the lobby, as if on a Cub Scout field trip. But their moods grow serious when, one by one, they are brought into the courtroom; nervous kids in dress shirts and ties and Nikes, innocent kids caught in the cross fire of warring adults.

Timid, their words on the witness stand are barely discernible. While cross-examining the boys, the woman's attorney impatiently taps his fingertips together. He places land mines to trip up witnesses who step in the wrong spot and, for those still unscathed, fires a machine gun of questions to crack their credibility.

Between sessions, one of the young witnesses looks at the stockpiled ammunition on the attorneys' tables, piles of notes and documents.

"This is a mess," says the little boy.

When the seven-day trial finally ends, the court reporter has typed the equivalent of 1,400 double-spaced pages. The judge has listened to about 30 witnesses. The attorneys have entered 110 pieces of evidence, everything from belts allegedly used for hitting to photographs of smiling father and son. The man and woman have spent about $35,000 in attorney's fees; one attorney charges $120 an hour, the other $170.

Two weeks after the trial ends, the judge, "with considerable trepidation," grants custody of the child to the mother and gives the father liberal visitation rights. In his decision, he mentions a recent case in which the state had to remove a child from the care of a mildly retarded man and woman. The couple had tried courageously to overcome their disabilities and be good parents, but it was not within their capacity. How sad, the judge points out, that two mentally sound people can hardly do better.

"For a variety of reasons, I hope never to see another case like this one," he says.

As the courtroom empties and the parties return to their new lives, you wonder how the same people who promised themselves to each other six years ago could become such bitter enemies. You wonder if it was all worth it; if divorce is, indeed, the great mender of wounds that it was hailed as back in the '70s. And finally, you wonder about the collateral damage of ending a marriage in the trenches of a courtroom trial.

What has this taught the older children about how adults solve family problems? And what will become of the three-year-old who, as the judge says in his decree, has been "ping-ponged" between two feuding parents?

The sad irony is this: The time and place to prove one's proficiency as a parent isn't during a divorce proceeding in front of a judge but in a marriage setting in front of the children themselves. For all the time, money, and energy that went into this trial, all it has really proven is the high cost of divorce—in money and human casualties.

In the end, the most profound statement of the trial has not come from the judge, from either attorney, or from the husband or the wife. Instead, it has come from the little boy who surveyed the scene and pronounced it "a mess." His comment was echoed by an adult witness of the carnage.

"This is worse than war," he said as people filed from the courtroom. "In war, at least you have a winner."

Letters of Love

IT WAS 1944 AND SHE WAS AWAY from home for the first time, having left the farm on the prairie of south-central Minnesota for nursing school in Minneapolis.

Each day, the dormitory's house mother would arrange the newly arrived mail alphabetically on the lobby coffee table. Marge would immediately look in the left-hand row—her last name began with a "B"—and, at least once a week, see it: a letter from her mother.

In a world where style has become paramount, it's often the substance in the shadows that's most inspiring. A 63-year-old woman. Her 85-year-old mother. And a commitment to a relationship. Two people linked by love and letters.

"Our closeness," Marge once told me, "has come from the words we've exchanged."

The two started writing when postage stamps cost three cents. In six different decades, in three states, spanning four wars and the death of both women's husbands, the letters have continued—thousands of them.

"You don't measure mom's letters by the page," Marge said. "You measure them by the pound."

Esther, Marge's mother, sometimes wrote about the early days when she and her husband were trying to survive the '30s on a farm, with two infant children.

"Before the Depression you *lived* life," she said. "Afterward, you *fought* it."

Kerosene lamps. Water fetched from a well. Hot summers. Cold winters. Drought. No car. And precious little money.

"I didn't even own a purse," said Esther.

But Marge remembered a different childhood. Not bliss, but a warm family, a high school class of 13, and a mother who shared the piano bench on Mills Brothers tunes.

"I didn't know we were so poor," she said.

At 18, Marge left for nursing school. "When she left for Minneapolis, it was like cutting off one of my arms," said Esther. "My husband would come in and I'd be crying and he'd wonder why. I'd tell him my little girl has left and I'm lonesome."

So, too, was that little girl. Thus began the letter writing. "The mailman would come down the road about nine o'clock every morning," said Esther. "I'd be thrilled to death if there was a letter from my daughter."

"Her letters kept me afloat," said Marge.

Soon, there were letters to Mom about a special boy Marge had met, later about plans for marriage, still later about her pregnancy. She eventually had three children. Esther came and stayed when Marge's children were born and when they were sick and her daughter needed help.

"She's always been there when I needed her," said Marge. "And I've had a lot of needs."

In 1962, after mother and daughter moved to Oregon, Esther's husband died of cancer. It wasn't the last time the disease would call on the family. In 1969, Marge had a mastectomy. Three years later, her husband died of cancer. Mother and daughter found themselves alone, together.

"It was a very tough time," said Marge.

After Marge moved five hours away, the two continued their letters. Marge wrote on weekends and mailed on Monday. Esther received on Wednesdays and wrote that night.

The letters included all sorts of topics, from the trivial to Marge's latest bout with cancer. "Life started with her and I can't imagine not including her in everything I do," said Marge.

She wrote about ten pages on a steno pad; her mom responded with at least a couple dozen. Sketches of happy faces and musical notes accompanied the words.

"She has a need to tell people things and I'm glad I can be there to meet that need," said Marge.

Someone once observed that a 20-year-old mother is 20 times as old as her child when the baby is 1. At 40, she's only twice as old. And at 80, she's only one-and-a-third times as old. By 1990, Esther and Marge had become more like good friends than mother and daughter, grown-up pals who, whether together or apart, have struggled through a Depression, disease, death, and the day-to-day challenges of life.

Why? Because they have been willing to be open and honest. Because they've built a mother-daughter friendship based on the nitty-gritty of real life instead of trading "all-is-fine" superficialities. And because on a clear September day more than half a century ago, before climbing on a Greyhound bus and leaving home, a daughter promised to write. And when she did, her mother always wrote back, each letter beginning the same way.

My dearest...

Part V

Courage:

Raising Your Sails

To change directions is a difficult tactic at best, and we're doomed to failure, destined to become a prisoner of the wind, if we attempt it in an ineffectual way.

Richard Bode, in *First You Have to Row a Little Boat*

SAILING, IN MANY WAYS, IS AN ACT of faith. Actually, a series of acts of faith: getting on board. Leaving the dock. Raising the sails. Trusting that when the boat begins to heel, the centerboard below will keep it from tipping. In each step, we trust in something beyond us. That is called faith—as Hebrews 11:1 says, "being sure of what we hope for and certain of what we do not see."

And nowhere is a sailor's faith tested more dramatically than when he dares to change directions, or come about: It is to sailing what taking off and landing are to flying, a crucial point when much can go wrong. But if your sailing destination is directly into the wind, which it often is, you can't get there by drawing a straight line from Point A to Point B and following it. A sailboat can't sail directly into the wind. Instead, you must zigzag, or tack, your way to that point.

To the non-sailor watching from afar, you may appear to be sailing a puzzling pattern. But you must stay the course. You must have the faith that even though your boat won't actually point directly toward the destination until the very end, there is, in Shakespearean terms, "method to this madness."

Risking Change

Likewise, in life, it's easy to wonder if such zig-zagging is necessary. Why must we live here if our desire is to live there? Why must we take this job if our dream job lies somewhere else? Why must I zigzag when I'd rather head straight for the target?

To change courses is to risk the known for the unknown. It's trusting that all you've read and been told and experienced is true—that if you alert the crew with a call of "ready about!" and push the tiller and let go of the jib sheets and shift from one side of the boat to the other, you will, after a few seconds of panic and pandemonium, find yourself headed in a new direction, comfortable in your position, and confident in the direction the boat is headed.

But so frightening is the prospect of deviating from one course to another that most people choose, instead, to stick to a tack regardless of whether it's getting them where they need to go. Rather than change, some would prefer to face all sorts of unnecessary danger. Likewise, some would rather stay forever becalmed, a state in which they're secure and comfortable—and yet, deep in their souls, know they're unfulfilled, having never experienced life at its deepest level.

"Superficiality is the curse of our age," writes Richard J. Foster in *Celebration of Discipline.*

If the beginning of change is coming face to face with where we are—indeed, *who* we are—then the avoidance of change often stems from our unwillingness to face such realities. Often, the workaholic never slows down because to do so is to have to contemplate himself, and that can be frightening. So he keeps plodding and plodding, believing that the business victories and stock options and vacations will somehow make it all worthwhile—taking risks every day in the pursuit of money but risking little for the pursuit of connections with God and people.

Only 15 percent of Americans say they'd be happier if they had nicer possessions, and yet we *live* as if we believe that deeply. I believe the discrepancy has to do with who or what we really trust; many who profess Christ as their hope seem to place that hope more firmly in the material world.

So for many, the courage to change involves leaving a place where we've been anchored a long time, a place that we once thought we belonged but realize now we don't. We all drop anchor somewhere, by design, default, or accident. We might anchor ourselves to money. Pride. Politics. Self. Sports. Shopping. Business. It might be a hobby. It might be an addiction. It might be an affair.

Then again, it might be something that looks quite virtuous on the outside—say, church—but ultimately becomes an impediment because we become fixed to it, and only it, and relationships get cast aside in our pursuit of it.

In short, we've dropped anchor in the wrong spot. Thoreau writes of "...anchors which have been lost—the sunken faith and hope of mariners, to which they trusted in vain."

Before some can set sail on a voyage to a new place, they must first lift an anchor that's kept them stuck in an old place. And that means taking a risk. But the greatest risk, I've come to believe, is not taking one. For just as the most efficient way for a sailor to get from Point A to Point B is through a series of zigzag tacks, so does life require us to be constantly changing—not simply for the sake of change, but for the sake of getting to where we need to get—and growing in the process.

So in our journey to lead a more fulfilled life, in which relation-ships—not stuff and status—rule the day, the fifth step is one that reaches deep within us all.

It lies deeper than the sensitivity required to understand where we are.

Deeper than the vision required to imagine where—and why—we need to get someplace new.

Deeper, even, than the strategy we implement to seek that new destination.

The fifth step in making any sort of life change is courage—the moral strength to venture, to persevere, and to withstand danger, fear, or difficulty. The guts to come about. To go in a new direction.

If strategy refers to planning the action you'll take to get from Point A to Point B, courage is the catalyst that makes that action happen. It is the impetus to hoist the sails. And above all, it is about overcoming fear.

Only Change Based in Truth Will Fulfill Us

Many of those who live lives of quiet desperation do so not because they're unable to change—not even because they're uncertain why or how they need to change, but because they're *afraid* to change.

It is an act of faith, this coming about. But faith is a freeing choice. Thor Heyerdahl, who sailed the *Kon-Tiki* to test the theory that ancient Peruvians could have navigated the Pacific Ocean in balsa rafts, was asked if he was frightened when he left sight of land and entered the open sea.

Not at all, he said. The greatest dangers lay along the shore, with the shoals and the rocks. Sailing into the expanse of the ocean, he said, brought him a sense of great relief.

But he couldn't have understood that truth unless he'd had the courage to leave the sight of land. Courage, you see, not only draws us out into the expanse, but teaches us something along the way, makes us more than we once were.

While on the short-term medical trip to the hinterlands of Haiti, I was bouncing along a bumpy road in a bus and talking with an American woman who had left the United States to become a full-time missionary in this, the poorest country in the Western Hemisphere.

"It must be hard," I said, "to leave a place with so much in order to live in a place with so little."

She thought for a moment, then smiled slightly, as if not to offend me.

"Actually," she said, "it's much harder going back to the United States than living here. Here, you're not tempted by all the trappings of materialism. But when I go back to the U.S. it's like sensory overload. I much prefer this."

I'd never thought of that. And neither had she—until she dared to leave America behind and find, at least for her, a sense of relief.

I believe that sense of relief has to do with entering the place of truth and leaving behind the superficiality of the world's lies—lies that suggest that fulfillment is a prestigious address or a salary increase or a home-theater setup away.

Recently, I read of a football coach being offered a new job thousands of miles away. He and his family, he said, were content where they were. "But they doubled my salary. When it came to my family, making this move was a no-brainer."

His logic is the same logic that's embedded in the American psyche, as if it were chromosomal: Only someone without a brain would pass up an opportunity to give up contentment where they were in order to make twice as much money somewhere else.

On the surface, many would probably agree. But looking deeper, maybe part of the discontentment in America today is precisely because of that kind of "brainless" thinking—that more money *necessarily* equals more contentment. That doubling your salary means doubling your pleasure. That bigger is always better. But I see no scriptural basis for it whatsoever.

Instead, I see Proverbs telling us that "wisdom is more precious than rubies" (8:11) and "wealth is worthless..." (11:4). I see Paul warning us in his first letter to Timothy that "the love of money is a root of all kinds of evil"(6:10). In Matthew 19:21 I see Jesus telling the rich young man who inquired about eternal life to "go, sell your possessions and give to the poor, and you will have treasure in heaven."

Christians in America too easily dilute Christ's teachings with the world's teachings, a subconscious attempt to justify their love for money and the things it will buy. And you can understand why, given that everywhere we look—TV, billboards, the Web— we're inundated with a money-is-all-that-matters message.

And here is where faith comes in.

Change Rooted in Faith

Faith is trusting in the word of God, not in the hype of the hucksters.

Faith is sailing toward destinations we cannot see.

In a sense, faith is rooted in repentance—in a willingness to turn from one course to another. A scary word, repentance, particularly to those who see God as some sort of a celestial cop instead of a loving savior. *Ax-murderers need repentance,* I think to myself, *not me.* But it's actually a freeing word. For at its root is the idea of turning *from* something—in this case, meaninglessness—*toward* something—meaning. Purpose.

> Do not conform any longer to the pattern of this world, but be transformed by the renewing of your mind. Then you will be able to test and approve what God's will is—his good, pleasing and perfect will.
>
> —Romans 12:2

To renew means to restore to freshness, vigor, or perfection. To make new spiritually. To revive. To begin again.

To transform means to change in composition or structure. To change in character or condition. In essence, to come about.

Not easy, this repentance stuff, particularly when pride enwraps our lives like pea-soup fog, obscuring the view of ourselves we need. I recently read a book by a fellow sailor who long ago cast off any idea that there lives a God who cares about a personal relationship with each of us; with a touch of pride, he writes of his decision to eschew any sense of the divine, instead choosing to "listen to the wind" and trust in "the journey."

Between the lines, what the book said to me is that broken relationships—including a shipwrecked marriage—have left him a lonely man and that his pride has prevented him from relating to the One he actually needs most.

I grieve for those who trust in nature more than the One who created it, the One who loves us so much that he promises to not leave us helpless at sea: "I will never leave you nor forsake you" (Joshua 1:5). And I grieve for those who trust in that same human perception that has, since the dawn of time, offered the world a painful pattern of greed, exploitation, and war—some of it done, sadly, by misguided individuals in the name of God, and much of it working against what God prizes so dearly: connections between people.

Courageous Change Moves Us Toward Others

Until we push the tiller and let loose the jib—until we purposely set a new course—we can't experience God's grace.

Courage is the catalyst to change.

It's what translates thought into action.

And quietly, beyond the headlines, I see things happening. People *are* taking courage. Making changes. Yelling "ready about!"

In the boomtime '90s, while America was fixated on a go-crazy stock market, enrollment at seminaries rose 10 percent, and more than half of this 10 percent was people 35 years and older, many of whom probably "had it all" and realized they really had nothing at all.

It takes courage to make a midlife course correction like that.

It takes courage to yell to the crew "ready about!"

It takes courage to give up life in the fast lane when that's the only speed you've ever traveled.

It takes courage, as a hairstylist in our church did recently, to give up a Saturday to cut the hair of the homeless for the day.

It takes courage, as my wife has done a handful of times, to fly to a Third World country and hold little children with scabies.

It takes courage, as a friend of mine did, to turn down a dream job in a big city, because he knew his family would ultimately pay the price for the the faster pace, demands of the job, longer commute, and higher cost of living.

It takes courage, as another friend plans to do, to take half a dozen at-risk youth camping and backpacking to help them turn their lives around.

It takes courage, as a few guys I know do, to play music before a couple of hundred homeless guys at a mission.

It takes courage, as a young deaf woman in our church did recently, to begin a signing class to teach others her language.

But, you see, all these steps have something in common: They're all about people making changes in order to better connect with people. They're about people investing in stuff that matters: relationships.

Sometimes when I'm singing a hymn in church, I'll look over and see what used to be only one woman signing to her daughter and see a half dozen people now signing the song, and I smile to myself.

It takes courage to change.

We can dream about a journey, mentally plan a journey, talk about a journey. But at some point, we must muster the courage to get in the boat and leave the dock.

"The winds of God are always blowing," goes the old Quaker saying, "but you have to hoist your sail."

Coming Home

Sometimes, awareness feels like an emotional knifing. Sharon will never forget her first personal point of insight. The teacher in her daughter's kindergarten class asked the students, "What does your mommy do?"

Sharon's daughter stood up, cleared her throat, and said words that got back to Sharon from another mother who'd been there.

"My mommy," she said, "makes money."

Sometimes, it takes more than one point of insight to inspire us to change courses in life.

At 41, the Seattle-area woman I once interviewed seemed to have it all: a house in the suburbs, a swanky car, and a management job with a worldwide computer firm.

"I was caught up in the American Dream," she said.

But beneath the façade, she was caught up in a nightmare. She and her husband were on the brink of divorce. And her daughter, by now an eighth-grader, was deep into drugs.

So Sharon did an uncommon thing: She quit a high-paying job to help save her family. She put a career on hold to reacquaint herself with a 14-year-old bundle of fascination and fear. She gave up the white-collar world of ladder-climbing for the blue-collar chore of rebuilding a crumbled relationship with her husband.

"I can always go back to work and take my Honda back on a trade," she told me, "but I'm not going to give up my kid and husband."

What intrigues me about her story is, this is not a woman who dreaded work and was looking for an out. This is a woman who thrived on it. She managed 17 software writers. She was good at what she did—and knew it.

But she carefully weighed the alternatives: She could keep pounding the corporate treadmill, losing sight of her family in the process. Or she could get off the treadmill to fix her fragmented family—and perhaps lose the chance to get back on.

"I was told by most of my peers that I'd committed professional suicide," she said. "There's not a man in the business who would take me seriously now."

Since she has left her job, only two colleagues have remained friends. The others, she says, have snubbed her as a quitter, as damaged goods, as weak. But that's all right, she says, because she's discovered, for the first time, life outside of work.

Now, Sharon realizes her daughter was not growing up with a mother, a role model, and a confidante—but with a stranger who carried a briefcase and occasionally came home to pop something in the microwave.

"We were a family in a hurry," she said. "For the first time, we now have an event that occurs every night between 6 and 8—we call it dinner. There's a sense of calm in the house. We do old-fashioned things like talk."

The transition was not easy for anybody, particularly Sharon's daughter. She had liked having the house to herself. She had liked what mom's salary meant to her wardrobe. But her drug problem signaled that freedom and big bucks were hardly the keys to contentment.

Sharon knew that quitting her job wouldn't imbue the home with Leave-It-to-Beaver bliss. "But my daughter needed to feel cared for. The drugs and alcohol were symptoms of a larger problem."

For the first time, Sharon learned who her daughter's friends were—and which ones were bad news. She opened the house to the responsible friends. And, along with her husband, set down some hard-and-fast rules for her daughter, penalizing her when they were broken.

Most of all, Sharon said, she just listened. And observed. Became aware, in other words. "Sometimes, you don't need to say anything, you just need to *be there*."

If she had taken the time to do that before, she says, she would have noticed the glazed look in her daughter's eyes when she was high on marijuana. She would have noticed when her daughter had boyfriend problems and needed someone to talk to.

In doing so, Sharon has become more than just someone who makes money. She is a mother—and proud of it. Her marriage is improving. And she has established a freelance editing business in her home.

What she's learned, she says, is that people can't have it all. "And I don't particularly like that idea," she admitted.

But a question kept coming back to nag her, a question that ultimately triggered her decision to quit work, a question that she had to face when struggling to reach the American Dream.

"I said to myself, 'At what cost?'"

The Road Less Traveled

WE MET LAST SUMMER, just beneath Little Belknap Crater in Central Oregon. I was hiking south on part of the Pacific Crest Trail. She was hiking north.

After a summer of too little exercise and adventure, I was feeling a little smug about my six-mile day hike; at 6,000 feet, I wasn't even into sort-of-thin air, but in my midlife mind I'd rationalized that I'd really accomplished something.

Then along came Laura.

"Where'd you start?" I asked.

"Mexico," she said.

I mentally gulped, hoping she wouldn't ask where I'd started.

"And, uh, where you headed?" I asked.

"Canada."

OK, so maybe this wasn't the time to boast that I'd just bagged Little Belknap. Laura Buhl, I'd soon learn, was hitting the 2,000-mile mark on this day. A 26-year-old University of Oregon graduate student, she planned to arrive at the Canadian border September 25, return to Eugene the next day, and start school the next morning.

She said it matter-of-factly, as if just notifying a roommate that she was headed out to get bagels and would be back at five. But I later learned she did exactly what she'd hoped to: walk 2,658 miles in 148 days and arrive on the day she predicted, a feat that seems as amazing to me as the *Eagle* landing on the moon's Sea of Tranquility after a 238,000-mile journey from Earth.

The world is full of Laura Buhls, people who accomplish amazing things with no thirst for fame or fortune. The problem is, the media caters to the rich and famous; thus, in 1999 while Buhl was quietly averaging 21 miles per day through the Mojave Desert, over 13,200-foot Forester Pass in California, and across the remnants of one of the heaviest snowfalls in Northwest history, the press was keeping track of multimillionaire athletes such as Latrell Sprewell.

Sprewell, a 29-year-old NBA star, is the guy who nearly choked his former coach to death during a practice session. But that didn't prevent him from landing a $9.1-million-a-year contract with the New York Knicks after Golden State traded him.

It's ironic that in September, as Buhl was trudging through obscurity to arrive on time, Sprewell was making headlines for not only failing to arrive at training camp on time—he was a week late—but for failing to tell his employers where he was. When he finally arrived—in a Mercedes-Benz that he'd recently driven onto a freeway from an exit ramp, broadsiding another car—he was asked why he hadn't checked in.

"That's what agents are for," he said.

Sprewell's approach to life is why I find Buhl's so inspiring; while he seems to have it all and appreciates so little, she has learned the secret of simplicity. The value of discipline.

"I've always been intrigued by the romance of the border-to-border trip," Buhl says. "Two borders. One trail. It's perfect."

In 1999, 270 people attempted the same journey, according to the Pacific Crest Trail Association. Fewer than 60 made it.

Buhl, carrying a 30- to 35-pound pack, walked much of the trip alone, beginning May 2. A typical day involved hiking from about 6 A.M. to 7 P.M., her record being 31 miles in a day.

"I don't consider myself hard-core," she says. "Some hikers walk 40 miles a day."

She had food mailed to pickup points along the way. She encountered two bears, seven rattlesnakes, about 7 trillion mosquitoes, 30- and 95-degree temperatures, 35 miles with no available water, rain, snow, and a desert windstorm that left her sunscreened face "feeling like sandpaper."

No animals hassled her, nor people for that matter; the most dangerous point was a stream crossing when she lost her footing and was nearly swept over a waterfall. ("Dear Mom and Dad, having a great time; no need to worry…")

Spring became summer. Summer became fall. And suddenly Buhl saw a 10-yard swath in the forest—the border between the United States and Canada—and knew she'd done what she set out to do. It was September 25, her predicted arrival date.

Her father met her and drove her home. She arrived back in Eugene, Oregon, at 10:30 P.M. the night before school started, caught some sleep, and made her 9 A.M. class—ironically, "Jog-Run."

To honor her, some friends bought Buhl breakfast. A few weeks later, the Knicks gave Latrell Sprewell a new contract: $61.9 million over five years.

Some people, it seems, know the price of everything and the value of nothing. And some people have learned that the best things in life aren't things.

Indeed, to hear Buhl talk about reaching that border or watching a Sierra Nevada sunset or being invited to join the Saltmarsh Family Reunion just past the California-Oregon line begs us to ask a question:

Between Sprewell and Buhl, who, really, is the richer of the two?

Easing the Misery Index

It's August in Mendenhall, Mississippi, where it's so hot that the local newspaper publishes what's called a "misery index." High temperatures and high humidity have sent the misery index soaring. And over the years, high rates of poverty and high rates of racism have sent the state's misery index soaring.

I am in Mendenhall on behalf of my Seattle-area church, which has linked arms with Mendenhall Ministries in an attempt to help bring hope to people who have little.

After playing a game of street baseball, I talk to an eight-year-old boy who has nine sisters and five brothers. He lives with his grandmother. His mother lives in a nearby city.

"I don't have a daddy yet," he tells me.

This is a place where a railroad track separates the white part of town from the black part of town, the latter a run-down area labeled The Quarters, so called because it's where slaves once were housed. The Quarters is a place that echoes the heartache from decades of discrimination. It's the kind of place that made a boy named Dolphus Weary fantasize about someday leaving it behind.

Weary was born the son of a sharecropper in southern Mississippi in 1945. He grew up in a house without running water, plumbing, or a father. He spent his days picking cotton and dreaming about what it was like on the outside.

He grew up in a time when black men were occasionally lynched, when three civil-rights workers were murdered in Mississippi, when the admission of a black student to the University of Mississippi triggered violent riots.

For Dolphus Weary, Mississippi was hopeless. And so his cotton-field fantasy was a small one: to get out.

And ultimately, that chance came. He graduated valedictorian of his high school class and was voted Most Likely to Succeed. He was offered a basketball scholarship at Los Angeles Baptist College. He and a friend were the first two blacks to graduate from the school.

At the time, Weary felt he had arrived. He had beaten the odds, triumphed over poverty and racism, proven the doubters wrong. His dream was unfolding. Now, he would get married, get a master's degree, settle in California, and live happily ever after, far from Mississippi and its misery index. He would embrace the life he'd never known. For once, Weary had a choice to do what he wanted to do, not what circumstances forced him to do.

His choice? To move back home.

In the movie *Trip to Bountiful,* an elderly woman feels compelled to return to the town where she had grown up, to remember what it had been like. In real life, Weary felt compelled to return to the town where he had grown up, to envision what it *could* be like.

And so a man who had beaten all sorts of odds to achieve the cultural equivalent of success gave it all up to return to the poorest county in Mississippi. At first, he wasn't even sure why he had returned; he only knew he must.

He prayed for direction, then prayed some more. And soon, the dream came: to help revitalize a place parched by time and circumstances. Something, he realized, had to be done to break this cycle of poverty, banish this specter of racism, bring light to this black hole of hopelessness. Somehow, Weary thought, the spiritual and social threads that Christ so perfectly intertwined had to be woven into this place.

Weary began by developing programs for youth that emphasized skills that students needed to get into college. A gymnasium and school were built. A church, farm, thrift store, health center, and law clinic were established.

Volunteers from churches around the country began trickling into Mendenhall to help, some on a short-term basis, others coming and never going back. A schoolteacher from Chicago became the school superintendent. An attorney with a graduate degree from Columbia University in New York gave up her chance for a six-figure income to help establish justice in a small town where there was little. A doctor from New York gave up the good life to bring comfort to Mendenhall's ill— and still found time to play the organ at Sunday-morning church.

Amazing things started happening. Eighteen-year-old youths destined to wind up working in a local factory or gravitating to big-city gangs instead started leaving for college. Weary was being asked to speak at churches around the country about how programs similar to Mendenhall Ministries could be established in other places. The icy wall between blacks and whites in Mendenhall slowly started melting; members of the First Baptist Church held a joint Easter celebration with the predominantly black Mendenhall Bible Church.

For Weary and those who joined his cause, the gospel had become not just a Sunday-morning add-on to their lives, but the thread that ran through every part of their lives. Not just a reason to establish "programs," but a way to heal the physical and spiritual lives of *people*. Not a free pass to "success," but an empowering force of compassion.

Rags-to-riches stories usually end with someone owning a Fortune 500 company or being elected governor or driving a Mercedes. This one does not. For true riches are measured not in dollars, but in devotion—to God and to people.

On my last day in Mendenhall, Weary drove me to the local hospital in his battered station wagon to proudly show me and some others his newborn son—a son who would grow up in a better world because his father chose to help ease the misery index rather than flee from it. Chose to invest in the stuff of life that really matters. Chose to give instead of receive.

Lilies of the Field

A YEAR AGO AT THIS TIME, my professional future fluttered like a sail in those wild and worrisome seconds of "coming about." I'd risen to the highest point in my career—the position of features editor of Oregon's second-largest newspaper. I supervised 12 people. I had, literally, the corner office in a new building.

I was making more money than I'd ever made in my life and receiving a yearly bonus to boot. I was comfortable and secure in a position that required little risk or vulnerability. My job, basically, was to manage people, which was sometimes rewarding and sometimes less fun than unclogging a garbage-disposal line. In either case, it was a steady tack, not one fraught with the risk of an unintentional jibe.

Then came a surprise: word that one of the paper's two staff columnists was retiring. I weighed the pros and cons of my current position and the columnist position—made one of those line-down-the-middle-of-the-page comparisons—and on paper, it came down to this:

If I applied for and got the columnist position, I would be giving up more than 10 percent a year in annual salary and a handsome yearly bonus. I would be moving from a corner office to a cubicle—like giving up a country estate for a downtown condo.

I would be giving up the anonymity of working safely behind the scenes for having to answer for every word I wrote—to an often-blustery readership that could make Oregon's storied 1962 Columbus Day Storm seem like nothing but an October breeze.

Everything on that sheet of paper screamed at me: Stay the course. But deep inside, I felt a tug to return to my first journalistic love: writing, which my current job did not afford. To challenge myself. To see if, in what many believe to be Oregon's most contentious community, I could somehow make a difference.

I prayed hard about whether to apply. Sought the advice of respected colleagues. And had many a long talk with Sally about what such a change could mean for me, and for us as a family.

Her mind was made up. "Go for it," she said. "I don't want you someday looking back and wondering, 'Could I have done that?' You know you can."

But, I countered, what about the pay cut? After eight years working part-time as a receptionist in a pediatrics clinic and with grown kids, Sally had recently quit to recharge her batteries at home, a move we never regretted but which was already pinching our finances. My book sales weren't exactly keeping pace with the Harry Potter line. And we had one son in college and a second who—Lord and an admissions director willing—would be starting soon.

In a practical sense, this was not the best time to be taking a pay cut.

But then, how practical, really, is faith? How practical was it for the fishermen, after Jesus' instruction to do so, to cast their nets in the same seas that had provided so little and have those nets come up full? How practical is it for the blind to see and the lame to walk?

I thought about worry—and about the birds and the lilies of the field, from a verse I'd seen on a dorm room window every morning as I walked to college classes two decades ago:

> Therefore I tell you, do not worry about your life, what
> you will eat or drink; or about your body, what you will
> wear. Is not life more important than food, and the body

more important than clothes? Look at the birds of the air; they do not sow or reap or store away in barns, and yet your heavenly Father feeds them. Are you not much more valuable than they? Who of you by worrying can add a single hour to his life?

And why do you worry about clothes? See how the lilies of the field grow. They do not labor or spin. Yet I tell you that not even Solomon in all his splendor was dressed like one of these. If that is how God clothes the grass of the field, which is here today and tomorrow is thrown into the fire, will he not much more clothe you, O you of little faith?

—Matthew 6:25-30

After reading these verses I was faced with a fairly threatening question: Do I *really believe* this? If not, then why believe anything Scripture has to say? But if I do, then why not trust His word and apply for the job?

I applied. So did dozens of other applicants from around the country. But I got the job. And have never regretted that decision to apply.

Not that this new course has been safe and comfortable and easy; not at all. I've been lambasted in letters to the editor. I've been ripped by callers on a talk-radio show. I've learned that, unlike the guy selling irrigation pipe at Home Depot, if I have a bad day 75,000 readers notice. I've learned that writing three columns a week, as a colleague of mine reminds me, is like running in front of a moving combine: lots of fun—until you trip just once.

Paying our bills each month has sometimes been challenging; at one point, we were $500 short on a college payment that needed to be made in two weeks. We've had to forgo some things we wanted to buy. We've once again put off replacing our rust-orange, oh-so-'60s carpet that we've wanted to replace since we moved into the house ten years ago. We've pushed back a planned 25th-anniversary trip down the East Coast. But we've survived. And most important, I think I'm where God wants me to be.

Looking back, I confess that one of the forces working against my applying for the job was a subtle cultural pressure I felt that suggested to climb *down* the corporate ladder was, well, un-American, a professional retreat. To take a pay cut was to fail my family. To give up a corner office was, well, just plain *wrong*.

Deep inside, I think I clung to this stubborn notion that to even apply was somehow a sign of failure, weakness, loss. Deep inside, I think it was far easier to aspire to be like the world's idea of a successful man than Christ's example.

I mean, look at Jesus—in many respects, He was everything our culture calls a loser: He was homeless. He never went to college, never got married, never had children, never even owned a camel or a donkey; He was nothing of what the world calls a "success."

But God's Word woke me up. While I consider myself patriotic, I read nothing in Scripture suggesting we're to conform to our culture—or any culture for that matter. In fact, I read very clearly that we are *not* to "conform to the pattern of the world," as Romans 12:2 says, but to "be transformed by the renewing of your mind."

All of which, when you attempt it, can seem rather spiritually heroic until you're facing a $500 college payment that's due in two weeks and you haven't a clue where the money is coming from.

In our family budget, my newspaper income generally keeps us afloat in terms of basic living costs, and my outside writing income pays for Ryan's college. But as I crunched the numbers late one summer evening, there was no freelance check on the horizon, no book royalties expected, no reserve account that we could draw from.

All we could do was pray—and resort to that less honorable tactic of forgetting about the payment, with the idea that it might somehow go away. Then came an unexpected letter from a publisher who, years ago, had expressed interest in a magazine piece I'd written.

Besides the letter was something that reminded me about the lesson of the lilies: a check for $500.

A Shaft of Sunlight

IT WAS, JACK HATFIELD WOULD LATER remember, the blackest night he's ever seen: late on a Sunday in the summer of 1983. Along with his wife, Susan, and three children—11, 9, and 7— he sat in the family's Chevrolet Malibu station wagon, a car packed tight with the stuff of their life, at a service station on the north edge of Bend, Oregon.

The Hatfields were moving from the small central Oregon town to Portland, on the other side of the Cascade Mountains. They had just come from a church send-off, where dozens of friends had hugged them good-bye. Where they had faithfully served for seven years. Where their children had been baptized.

Now they sat in a car at a gas station, soon to drive away from a life that seemed to have it all. Jack had been poised to become district manager of five retail clothing stores. They'd just bought their dream house on a half-acre where you could sit on their back deck and see nothing but pine trees and buttes and mountains. They had security, a flock of friends, and a certain degree of prestige, which they hardly wore on their sleeves but which, deep inside, offered a certain quiet assurance.

And they were giving it all up.

And for what, really? For Jack, at age 32, to go to seminary for four years while the family grew poorer and poorer. For a small-town family to live in a city with nearly half-a-million people. For a family used to crisp, blue-sky winters and the warmth of friends to live in a rental in a place where they knew absolutely no one, a place known for long, rainy winters.

Jack felt a loneliness he couldn't describe. And flat-out fear. He kept his eyes forward so the kids wouldn't see his tears.

As he started the car and drove away from all that he'd had, he remembers having had one distinct thought: *What have I done?*

☾   ☾   ☾

LIFE IN AMERICA WORKS LIKE THIS: You grow up. You go to college. You get married. You have 1.5 kids. You get a job. You climb the ladder. You buy a house. You buy a bigger house. You climb, climb, climb. But every now and then, one of those climbers dares to look where he's been and where he's going and realizes something: He's on the wrong ladder.

Jack Hatfield was one of those climbers. I attended the same church he did in the late '70s and early '80s. He was not your typical type-A business zealot. In fact, he always seemed far too low-key to be the manager of one of the area's largest retail clothing stores. And part of this may have been that, deep inside, his heart lay elsewhere.

The decision to become a pastor didn't present itself to Jack in a lightning bolt. It came gradually, from a growing sense that, although he enjoyed his job, he basically helped people change on the outside—but what really mattered, he'd decided, was on the inside. In dealing with customers, employees, and vendors, he found conversations naturally turning not to the physical but to the spiritual side of life.

At church, he took a fledgling "Young Marrieds" class and breathed new life into it. The class grew in size and maturity, and Jack found the experience fascinating.

Hurting people began seeking him as a source of counsel. Once, he got a phone call from a single mother at church; her 5-year-old son had fallen out of a tree onto his head—on asphalt. Church pastors were unavailable. Would he come to the hospital?

Jack had no training. No experience. No credentials. But when he showed up at the hospital, he felt little fear. Instead, as he prayed with the woman and cried with the woman, he sensed this was where he belonged.

At work, he found himself softly weeping one day and perceived God saying to him, *You will be a pastor someday.* He remembers responding, *You must have the wrong guy. But if this is Your will for my life, I am willing.*

Well, sort of. A year later, he was driving to Portland to check out Western Baptist Seminary. Somewhere in the mountains, he prayed, "God, I just want to do ministry, not study it. I want to help people come to know the truth. I don't want to spend four years in an ivory tower experience, locked away from people who need more of You."

Again, he began crying for seemingly no reason. This time, he sensed God telling him that he should consider it a privilege to spend four years studying about Him. And Jack's crying suddenly ceased. He knew that was what he must do.

Friends and family, including his parents, affirmed that it was the right thing to do. But Susan?

"God may have called you to be pastor," she told Jack, "but He hasn't called me to be a pastor's wife." And she was convinced she wasn't ever going to get that call. Her line was, as it were, permanently busy.

After all, there was the new dream house on half an acre. The security. The friends. Cutting their own firewood. A zillion stars, with no city lights to intrude.

Why disrupt the kids' lives, moving them to some place where nobody knew them? And besides, this wasn't part of the deal: She'd married a businessman, not a pastor. Why should she accept his midlife change of direction? Why should she give up a secure future, complete with stock options, to train for a sometimes-thankless job that didn't pay too well in a city she didn't know or have any desire to know?

Then, came—no, not a bolt of lightning—but a shaft of sunlight. Months later, Susan was sitting in a Sunday school class when she saw it. She looked out the window where that sun was coming from and, for the first time, saw the wider possibilities, the reality that God might not only have something different planned for them, but something better. She understood, for the first time, that she didn't have to be a "pastor's wife" at all. She simply needed to be God's and let Him use her as He saw fit.

Thus did they find themselves leaving a gas station on that Sunday night, headed for who-knew-what.

(((

LIFE IN THE MOVIES HAPPENS LIKE THIS: Someone makes a decision to turn his life around, and presto, it happens with the no-mess swiftness of a microwave oven. I was once cold, but now I'm hot. Was lost, but now I'm found.

So why, then, did Jack find himself sitting at a clunky study desk in the hallway of a $405-a-month rental, exhausted from schoolwork and life in general, crying again? He'd never felt so lonely.

The first Portland church the Hatfields tried wasn't nearly as good as the one they'd left in Bend. On their initial visit, Jack and Susan walked into a Sunday school class and saw two empty chairs, as if they were meant for them. "Why don't you sit over there?" suggested a woman, pointing to seats far away.

After the service, Jack and Susan got talking to a young woman; this was encouraging—for a moment. She'd been a seminary student's wife; after her husband had graduated, he'd thanked her for supporting him by presenting her with divorce papers. Jack and Susan left that morning feeling totally defeated.

Jack was struggling with school; his first class, with 16 students, included three men who already knew Greek, several who had already been pastors, and a number who had been to Bible school. And then there was Jack, the former clothing-store manager, the misfit, the "C" student.

But the pain went even deeper. To help make ends meet, Jack had gone looking for a part-time job; he had the grand idea to use his retail-management experience to become a consultant for small businesses. He went to five stores. The result? Five rejections.

Sitting in that hallway—what, he wondered, was he doing with an office in a hallway anyway?—he wanted desperately to call someone or go see someone, but he didn't know anyone who'd care to listen.

He'd hear of the latest cruise friends back in Bend were taking and feel a sense of envy. He'd open up the latest bill—a bill that wouldn't have fazed him back in Bend—and wonder where the money was going to come from to pay it. He'd look out his window and see not central Oregon's high-desert blue sky but endless clouds the color of Malt-O-Meal.

Change asks a price; but if made for the right reasons, it also pays dividends. Three years after their move, the second Portland church the Hatfields attended had a bitter split between people who wanted to change and conform more strictly to Scripture and people who didn't. It got so bad that one usher was encouraging people *not* to present offerings, as a means of driving out the pastor. Seventy-five of the 200 people left the church. The pastor later resigned.

A search committee turned to Jack: Would he consider throwing his hat in the ring? A few months later, with an almost unanimous vote of the congregation, the fourth-year seminary student was chosen to be the new pastor at Evangel Baptist Church.

As the months and years unfolded, Jack and Susan started seeing the dividends roll in. Started realizing what an utter privilege it was to focus your lives on something as worthy as helping people better understand the Creator of the universe. Started realizing how the struggle to start over had drawn them closer together, how they'd become partners in a way that couldn't have happened in the clothing business. Started seeing the wonder of their three children grounding their lives in the things that mattered. Started realizing the beauty of living life at gut level.

Jack held people's hands as they died. Wept with parents whose only child committed suicide. Rejoiced in marrying people. Celebrated as a flat-lined marriage was brought back to life.

Meanwhile, Susan was his partner in nearly all that he did.

Theirs was an inner-city church, not in one of Portland's finer neighborhoods. But this was where the church was and this was where it would stay. When Jack took over, the collateral damage of the split was everywhere. People were wounded. People who had stayed at the church were being shunned by those who had left. Even some husbands and wives disagreed with each other about whether to stay.

Jack's message was simple: If this church was going to survive, it needed to become a church of unity, not disunity. Not that everyone had to agree on every issue; unity didn't mean unanimity on every issue. People needed to learn to appreciate one another's differences. But they needed to do so in a context of oneness.

The church didn't grow large in numbers, but it did grow strong in unity. The church became an extended family of the Hatfields'. There were suburban churches that had nicer buildings, bigger congregations, more money. But Jack and Susan realized geography didn't matter; they grew to love the church, regardless of where it was located and regardless of what it had been through.

Once a year, the family camps for a week near Mount Hood to get its outdoor fix. But returning to their old hometown no longer brings back pangs of regret; over the years it has grown from a small, one-size-fits-all community to a sort of Palm Springs with pine trees, a vacation mecca that no longer feels like home.

On visits back to Bend, they'd see that old gas station and Jack would remember the night he sat there and thought to himself: *What have I done?*

He's done what he needed to do, he's long since realized. Seventeen years later, when you ask him what he gave up, he'll tell you, "Nothing." And what has he gained?

"Everything."

Part VI

Grace:

Trusting the Wind

O Lord, have mercy,
Thy sea is so large,
And my ship is so small.

Breton fisherman's prayer

LATE ONE AFTERNOON, AFTER I'D MET the first of my three-times-a-week column deadlines; after I'd plowed through four dozen e-mail messages; after I'd listened to a reader chastise me about my narrow-mindedness when it comes to social protest (I'm anti–car smashing); after I'd read the letter from a book editor telling me she wouldn't be using a particular story of mine after all; after learning that tuition at my son's college was going up nearly $1,000; after I'd run some errands; after I'd worked my way through some freeway traffic—after all this, I arrived at the lake.

I knew where I was—caught in the clutches of life's demands—and knew where I needed to be: on this little boat in this big lake. So I rigged *At Last*, plotted my course, and cast off.

Matthew 14:13 tells us about a time that Jesus "withdrew by boat privately to a solitary place"; He did this kind of thing fairly often, going off by Himself. Don't get me wrong—I'm not making any personal comparisons here—but this lake is my solitary place. This is the place that reminds me to "Be still, and know that I am God" (Psalm 46:10). This is where I will sometimes pray and take out a notepad and write. Or do that something that so often gets lost in the cultural clutter: think.

Sometimes, I anchor in a small cove, a protected place where grebes dive and pop up like submarines on training missions, and swim. I'll be backstroking and see the white mast against the blue sky and hear the water gently lap against the hull and smell that wonderful lake-water smell that chlorine will never match—and think of how undeserving I am of all this goodness.

It is too perfect. It is a gift. Undeserved favor. In a word, *grace*. And I'm convinced that grace ties together every part of life's journey: awareness, vision, purpose, strategy, and courage. Picture five boats tied together for the annual Independence Day fireworks over the lake. Grace is the line that keeps them together as one.

Grace Connects Us and Moves Us

If we're called, above all, to glorify God by connecting with Him and with those around us—if this is our reason for living—then grace must do the connecting.

God, you see, loves us in a way the world does not: unconditionally. Without an agenda. With no fine print that says He loves us now, but it's only an introductory-rate offer that will change after six months, based on prime interest rates. With no campaign promise that He'll love us, but only if we vote for Him or give to His campaign fund. With no prenuptial agreement that says He'll love us, but just in case, let's put together a contract.

Grace promises that eternal life awaits not those who live a perfect life, say so many Hail Marys, never miss church, or donate so much money. It awaits those who *believe* with childlike faith.

Led Zeppelin was wrong; there is no stairway to heaven. We can't work our way up some mythical set of steps. There is, instead, a gift that we can accept—or reject.

"It is by grace you have been saved, through faith—and this not from yourselves, it is the gift of God" (Ephesians 2:8).

Grace means that no matter how poorly we're skippering the boat, God validates our worth. It is absolutely, positively, un-American; this, after all, is the country that teaches there is no such thing as a free lunch. But God's love makes an exception.

"I do not at all understand the mystery of grace," author Anne Lamott writes in *Traveling Mercies*, "only that it meets us where we are but does not leave us where it found us."

Exactly! It takes us somewhere. It motivates us to move from the place where we are to the place we need to be. It is the gentle wind that fills our sails, the breath of heaven, unseen but always at work. Winds of grace.

> *He makes the clouds his chariot*
> *and rides on the wings of the wind.*
> *He makes winds his messengers.*
> —Psalm 104:3-4

Without winds of grace, we're easily motivated by ill winds:

- The winds of legalism. (Our life choices are based on dogmatic rules and regulations that honor rituals, not relationships).

- The winds of greed. (Our life choices are based on a you-scratch-my-back philosophy that places self, not others, at the heart of every decision.)

- The winds of fear and guilt. (Our life choices are based on the assumption that if I don't act in a godly manner then God or my parents or my culture might *get* me.)

- The winds of popular opinion. (Our life choices are based on what others do or think.)

When we're guided by the freeing winds of grace, however, we're more likely to make good choices—not out of guilt or greed or legalism, but out of gratitude. Gratitude for the grace God showed us when He sacrificed his Son so "whoever believes in Him shall not perish but have eternal life" (John 3:16).

The material world works another way. It says: If you use this product, you will be popular. If you live in this neighborhood, you have arrived. If you win this award, your worth is validated. The material world demands that you *do* something to earn favor.

God doesn't work this way. His grace is a gift. There's nothing we can do to make God love us more. There's nothing we can do—or can have done—to make God love us less. And when we accept this—not just nonchalantly agree, intellectually, that it's true, but hide it in our very hearts—it fills our life sails with a cleansing breeze.

What the Gift of Grace Does

Grace inspires us to give back because we were given *to*.

It frees us from seeing ourselves as pitiful pawns in a big-life game like TV's *Survivors*, our sole aim to use others for our own benefit. We realize that we've been called to need others and to meet the needs of others, not to use others. People around us become our neighbors, not "The Competition." Compassion, not control, becomes the goal.

It compels us to seek forgiveness of others when we've wounded them—and to forgive others when they've wounded us. When realizing that we've been forgiven by God, we more willingly do the same with others.

It encourages us to set our vision far beyond the superficial standards of the world. Instead of investing in only ourselves, we invest in something greater than ourselves.

It protects us, like a harbor in a storm. "You are my hiding place," says the Psalmist. "You will protect me from trouble and surround me with songs of deliverance" (Psalm 32:7).

It motivates us to not drink the water of the world, which leaves us thirsty again, but to drink Living Water, which quenches that thirst.

It guides us in the goals we set, the choices we make, the courses we take. If we accept the gift, if we've been saved by grace and granted everlasting life, then we needn't hoard treasures on earth. That, ultimately, is the Good News: that we needn't toil and strain to somehow *win* this earthly battle. Thanks to God, we've already won, which allows us to live with a far deeper sense of purpose than trying to meet some culturally imposed standard of success.

It supplies us the courage we need to struggle against the cultural currents. "If God is for us, who can be against us?" (Romans 8:31).

It saves us from running aground on the shoals of superficiality, our lives focused on earthly trivia instead of heavenly treasure. "The sorrows of those will increase who run after other gods" (Psalm 16:4).

Finally, it completes us, makes us whole, filling the emptiness in our hearts with that God-shaped piece that was missing.

True Need Is Willing to Receive Grace

So why, then, with all this available, do we often fail in connecting with God and others? Why do we continue to live in—and often contribute to—a world of takers rather than givers? Why do those who say they believe in this grace look so much like those who do not believe in this grace?

Because believing and *acting* on that belief are two different things. When I teach about writing profiles on people, I tell my students it's important to hear what your subject *says* about his or her life. But if you really want to understand the essence of that person, see what he or she does in life. Because what someone *does* with his or her time, talent, energy, and resources reflects what that someone really values—regardless of what they say.

We want so badly to control the winds, but the fact is, we don't; we only control the sails. And understanding that—humbling ourselves—leads to being blessed. "Blessed are the poor in spirit, for theirs is the kingdom of heaven" (Matthew 5:3).

Who is blessed? Not those who rumble through life with the notion that they know all and need nothing. Not those who take pride—even a subtle pride—in "having it all." Not those Pharisees among us who "love the place of honor at banquets and the most important seats in the synagogues."

Instead, those who are blessed are *those who know their need.* In the Gospels of Matthew, Mark, and Luke, Jesus' warnings about wealth nearly all come with the same concern: that it will give us a false sense of security, that we'll allow it to become, in essence, our god; that it will replace Him.

"The proof of spiritual maturity is not in how pure you are but in your awareness of impurity," writes Philip Yancey in *What's So Amazing About Grace?* "That very awareness opens the doors to grace."

John Newton had no need for grace. He loved the sea but despised the One who created it, not to mention practically everyone who lived and breathed. At age 24, the mid-eighteenth-century English sea captain was a slave trader who plied the waters of rebellion and debauchery. So hated was he by even his own crew that once, when he grew ill and was nearly starving to death, they refused to help him. Only the mercy of the slaves on board, who took pity on him and shared their meager portions, kept him alive.

Then, awareness: Amid a frightening storm, he read a book by a Dutch monk, Thomas à Kempis, *The Imitation of Christ;* he saw, for the first time, his vileness. For the first time, he had—in Yancey's words—an "awareness of impurity."

Vision: He realized, for the first time, that he needed what God offered.

Purpose: He realized, for the first time, *why* he needed what God offered, because his life had been a meaningless pursuit of self-gratification and other-exploitation.

Strategy: While on a small island off the coast of North Africa, he walked to a secluded part of the island away from his crew, where, as his journal says, "I cast myself before the Lord to do with me as He should please" and begged His forgiveness.

Courage: He gave up the security of his old life as a slave trader, went home to England, married, and became a desk clerk. Ultimately, he became a pastor in the small village of Olney.

It was there, in 1779, that Newton and the poet William Cowper wrote hundreds of hymns, including the one that stands as an anthem of the ultimate step in life change: accepting God's grace.

> *Amazing grace! how sweet the sound,*
> *That saved a wretch like me!*
> *I once was lost, but now am found,*
> *Was blind, but now I see.*

> *'Twas grace that taught my heart to fear,*
> *And grace my fears relieved;*
> *How precious did that grace appear*
> *The hour I first believed!*

> *Through many dangers, toils and snares,*
> *I have already come;*
> *'Tis grace hath brought me safe thus far,*
> *And grace will lead me home.*

Grace Makes the Ultimate Connection

Nearly 200 years later, another sailor found himself weary and worn, in the midst of a storm that threatened to end his life.

His name was Robin Graham.

When the teenager's round-the-world adventure was over, he realized that for all its grandeur it did not fill the emptiness in his heart. So distraught was he with life that, one night, he walked to the end of a dock with a gun in his hand and made ready to end it all—until his wife intervened.

But what ultimately saved him wasn't his wife. Nor was it some bigger, bolder adventure, a fancier boat, or a nine-to-five job. What saved him was the same thing that saved John Newton: amazing grace. Depressed, convinced he was, as a young husband and father, a complete failure, feeling ashamed for having wrecked a car while driving drunk, "convinced I was worthless," Robin Graham raised his sails to the winds of grace, opened his heart to the One behind those winds.

The journey he and wife Patti have been on since that time has included plenty of storms, but as they bounced from what they describe in the book *Home is the Sailor* as "fanatical" legalism to spiritual self-sufficiency, they ultimately reached the place they belonged.

"We discovered that, in keeping ourselves distant, we became more and more vapidly self-centered," wrote Robin. "We have learned that living for oneself, no matter how pious one might be, becomes a totally unfulfilling lifestyle. And complacency spells death to the spirit."

Grace, you see, goes beyond rules, regulations, and religion. Grace, at its essence, is about a relationship—between the Maker of the sea and those of us who sail it.

Time on Earth

I WAS 23 AND HAD BEEN MARRIED less than a year when I got the phone call. It was a Sunday night. Come quickly, said a hospital chaplain, your mother is dying.

Why does it take death to remind us what's important about life? Why does it take months, sometimes years, to understand grace, to see it unfold before us, bit by bit, like an 800-page novel instead of some skywritten message that, boom, is just *there?*

I remember the three-hour drive, over the Cascade Mountains, into a March snowstorm so mesmerizing that I would momentarily forget I was on a road at all and think I was in some sort of dreamland, some gigantic snow globe that someone had just shaken really, really hard.

Only this was no dream. It was a nightmare. My mind faded back and forth between past and present, like an automatic-focus video camera alternating between background and foreground.

My folks had been cross-country skiing, the chaplain had said. My father had been driving. Apparently he'd fallen asleep at the wheel and the car had hit a towering fir tree.

When I was young, she had these glasses that looked like the tail fins of our '59 Chevrolet Impala. But through those glasses she saw that people were important. From the start, she'd been my biggest cheerleader. When I was seven, I wrote a Santa Claus poem whose misspelled-word percentage was higher than any major leaguer's hitting percentage since baseball began, and which contained such wonderfully logical lines as, "So if you see him, be sure you do not see him." My mother thought it was the finest poetry since Shelley's and sent it to the local newspaper. They printed it. My journalism career was born.

You want to believe there's been some mistake. Like the relatives waiting in the airport after a jet has gone down, you don't wish bad fortune on others, but you hope that the airline's public relations coordinator quietly takes you aside and says your loved one is safe; the body was mistaken for someone else's. You imagine that happening. But you know it won't. You're driving into a blizzard and feeling numb.

She was nutty in a good sort of way. When I was 19, she showed up at a "Turkey Bowl" pickup football game I was playing in. She was dressed in her 1942 Corvallis High rally uniform. She made life fun. She made this huge, round coffee table for our family's beach cabin out of quarter-size river rock. She used tiles in the middle to make a design of a giant steelhead fish, the kind my father loved to catch in the Yachats River. The thing took up the entire living room and weighed about as much as Plymouth Rock. We joked that it was a giant paperweight that kept the cabin from being blown away in winter storms. But that was our mom: the one who kept our family from blowing away. Our anchor.

My father was OK, the chaplain had said. "Just some bumps and bruises," I told Sally. My mother, 48 at the time, was not. No head injuries. No broken bones. But the seat belt had ripped into her stomach. Lots of internal bleeding. Drive carefully, the chaplain said, but get here quickly.

What worried her most was that we wouldn't get a camping spot. Other than that, I don't remember her all that uptight, unless my father had gone and done it again—involved some sort of kitchen utensil in the

*building of a boat. I remember her telling my sister and me
one night that the four of us were going to Disneyland in
the summer, the first and only time our family would go.
The next morning I woke up and she was crying. I thought
she was crying because the trip had fallen through or
something. But she was crying because she'd just heard that
my father's dad, Papa Bill, had died.*

My wife Sally told me it was going to be OK. Then: "Are you
sure you don't want me to drive?"

I'm fine, really, I'd say. But nobody is fine whose mom is
dying. Sometimes one of us would just break into audible
prayer. Sometimes one of us would comment on something.
But mainly we drove in silence through the snow.

*We went to an Episcopal church when I was growing up. I
was too young to really understand what it all meant, the
stained glass, the black-and-white robes, the Nicene Creed.
My mom always looked real serious in church. Sometimes
she would cry and I would think: She really believes this
stuff. I wasn't so sure I did.*

Traffic was light, almost nonexistent. There were no tire
tracks in the snow to give us perspective, no taillights to follow.
It was like nobody had gone this way before. It was like I was
the first one to ever have a mom who was dying, though I
knew I wasn't.

You think strange thoughts at a time like this. You want to
say: Hold it, God. Hold everything. She's got to live so, in a few
years, when Sally and I have children…God, she would be such
an awesome grandmother…

*The worst thing I remember her doing was one Christmas
Eve. I was pouting, which I know the song says you
shouldn't do at Christmastime. And when I pouted my
nose got red and she would say, "Is that Rudolph I see?" as*

*in Rudolph the red-nosed reindeer. I hated that. The best
thing she ever did was mention the girl up the street and
how she sure was cute and maybe I should ask her out. I
was 18. Nobody who's 18 wants to ask out a girl his mother
has recommended. I waited a few months, then let it be my
idea. Later, I married her.*

The girl up the street sat next to me as we approached the
hospital. We were in the Willamette Valley now and the snow
had turned to rain. I remember how the red emergency sign
stood out in the darkness, a beacon of horror, not hope. I'd
seen signs like that all my life and had never given them much
thought. They were meant for someone else. Now the sign was
meant for me.

We met the chaplain. My father was standing there, his arm
in a sling and Band-Aids on his bruised face. He looked more
serious than I'd ever seen him, dazed, really. "Hiya, Bob," he
said. "We've got a tough one on our hands."

My mother looked dead. She was pale and still and had all
these tubes going in and out of her. My sister, Linda, and her
husband, Herb, were there. We sat in the private waiting room
and cried.

A doctor explained the situation. "The next 24 hours are
critical," he said. There was nothing for us to do. Everything
was blurry. We drove to a motel and tried to sleep. Days of
waiting. "Not out of the woods yet," the doctor would say in a
hushed tone.

She was conscious, but couldn't talk with all the tubes in
her. I held her hand and she squeezed it tight. Her eyes grew
watery. Mine, too.

Surgeries. More surgeries. The problem, the doctor
explained, was nourishment. They were trying to reconfigure
her intestines so food could get through her system.

Days of waiting. Weeks of waiting. Trips over the mountain every weekend, sometimes during the week. Letters. Phone calls. Daily progress reports from my father and my sister. Daily lack-of-progress reports as well.

Weeks become months, months became seasons. Spring became summer, summer became fall. Finally, just before Christmas Eve, nearly nine months after the accident, my mother walked into her house for the first time since she had left on that cross-country ski trip.

That Christmas was nearly 25 years ago.

I don't remember a single present I received that night.

I don't remember what the Dow Jones average did that day.

I don't remember what my net worth was.

What I remember is a broken family made whole again.

What I remember is a woman who'd nearly died being very much alive.

What I remember is that as our little family gathered in this living room, I felt touched by grace, forever branded with a neon "Emergency" light reminding me that time on earth is precious and we dare not waste a moment of it.

Traveling Light

In my mind, I try trading places with the Springfield, Oregon, parents whose children, in 1998, became the targets of 15-year-old gunman Kip Kinkel.

I remember that day: walking into the newspaper building where I work and having a frantic receptionist hand me a phone call. A kid was calling while locked in a room at Thurston High, about five miles from our office; a fellow student was on a shooting rampage.

I imagine that we'd never moved from the place on Camp Creek Road and how my youngest son would have been a Thurston High freshman that morning. And how he quite likely could have been in that cafeteria.

I imagine what it would have been like to find out he'd been shot, as 26 other students had been. Two died.

I imagine, 18 months later, standing in a courtroom and being allowed to say whatever I wanted to the young man who had tried to take my son's life.

"I forgive you" are not the first three words that come to mind.

And yet lost in the drama of this sentencing hearing—lost in the flurry of "I hate you" and "Why haven't you been destroyed?" bullets aimed at Kip—that's what a handful of victims and parents of victims said.

Among them was Jody Hardenbrook, a man whose then-freshman daughter, Jaclyn, was wounded in the arm. She left home a month later and has been living on the streets since. Though the family was struggling before the shooting, Hardenbrook believes the incident pushed his daughter over the edge.

Nevertheless, when given his chance to speak, Hardenbrook told Kinkel, "We love you and forgive you."

Could anything be as hard as forgiving someone who killed, or tried to kill, someone you loved? But in terms of healing, could anything be as necessary?

"The process of forgiving is in the victim's best interest," says Debra Whiting Alexander, a trauma consultant who has worked with the Thurston victims since the May 1998 shootings that killed two and left 24 wounded. "When you're consumed by hate, all you are is hate. Eventually it eats up everything left inside you."

But here's a warning for those of us who can only imagine what it must be like for the victims: It wasn't our kid. It wasn't us. We weren't there. And we need to be patient with those who were.

"People need to reach the point of forgiveness in their own time and in their own way," says Alexander, author of the book *Children Changed by Trauma*. "It's a very hard thing to do; it usually doesn't happen easily, or all at once. And being a homicide survivor is like no other experience you can have. It's natural to hold on to incredible anger and resentment."

What's more, to forgive—to give up resentment against someone—also asks a price. Some see it as letting an attacker off the hook, a betrayal to the victim, an in-your-face snub to justice itself.

"There were people who wouldn't even talk to me after I made the statement," says Hardenbrook.

Alexander says people often misunderstand forgiveness. "It doesn't mean removing the blame or forgetting what happened or not still wishing for justice," she says. "It means choosing to let go of vengeance and hate."

It means offering grace to people who don't deserve it.

Occasionally, you see it played out in the news. In 1983, Pope John Paul II met and forgave the man who shot him. In

1999, in Wyoming, the father of murder victim Matthew Shepard said he would never forgive convicted killer Aaron McKinney—and yet spared the man's life by brokering a deal to waive the death penalty.

In 1997, Art Gallegos Sr., whose son and another man were shot at a beer party near the city where I live, told those at the memorial service that he had forgiven the murderers.

"In a way, if you hang on to it, the perpetrator still has the power—he's still impacting you in a negative way," says Alexander. "And what victims need to be able to say is: I'm not going to hand him any more of myself on a silver platter."

In 1980, Monte Leighton was a senior at Marshfield High in Coos Bay, Oregon, when his parents were murdered by a neighbor, who then killed two others. The murderer, it turned out, was the father of a good friend of Leighton's.

Leighton, now 37, forgave the man who killed his parents. He even served as best man at the wedding of the murderer's son. "What I would tell people is that it's a journey," says Leighton, now a pastor in Tacoma. "At the beginning, there was anger, nightmares. I'd dream I tracked the man down and shot him. But now, I've released it."

Leighton made a symbolic gesture out of letting go, not only for his father's and mother's murderer, but for others who had hurt him over the years. He went to the beach, found some rocks, named each for a different situation, then cast them into the sea.

"It was hurting me too much to pack those rocks along each day," he says.

As we seek to make relationships our priority, the lesson of grace may be the most important. Sailboats sail best when they're light.

Like Leighton, we dare not bring with us rocks that will impede the voyage.

Tale of Two Sailors

It is summer. Six o'clock on a Tuesday morning and the house is still and cool. In a few hours the cars in my neighborhood will start zipping by and my college- and high-school-age sons will sleepily descend the stairs they once sledded down as kids. The cats will want out and Sally will turn on the radio to hear the weather report. I will begin thinking of my newspaper column deadline. The July heat will start intruding on the coolness.

For now, though, I sit here in my house and think of my wife, who sleeps down the hall. Next month we will celebrate 25 years of marriage, and I haven't stopped enough to ponder the significance of that.

My oldest son is 21, the age I was when I got married. My youngest son is 18, the age I was when I met Sally.

Where does the time go?

In the summer of '72, when I first met Sally, one of the first photographs I took of her was of her sitting on a sailboat in the middle of Fern Ridge Lake. It was, I admit, a risky second date—as a rookie sailor to take a girl you hardly knew on such an adventure; easier, really, to see a movie. And it did not get off to a good start when, trailering the boat to the lake, an hour from home, I missed a turnoff and had to pull into a farmhouse driveway along a fairly busy road.

But at least I know she didn't fall in love with me because of my trailer-backing ability, which I displayed for the 20 longest minutes of my life. I had never backed up a trailer in my life, a fact that Sally quickly realized. When we eventually got to the lake, light winds nudged us to the middle, then stopped altogether. That's when the rain began, followed by blustery wind, followed by the boom swinging around and cracking Sally in the head, followed by laughter that wouldn't come to an end.

Not exactly a dream date. But you learn more about someone in the hard times than in the easy times, and I learned something about Sally that day. I learned that she was the kind of person you'd want to be with if you suddenly found yourself becalmed in a rainstorm and needed someone to help you hand-paddle to shore, which is a lot of what life seems to be about.

Summer was over; autumn was coming. It was the wrong time to be falling in love; I would leave for college in two weeks. But it was only the wrong time in a practical, human sense. In other, deeper realms, it was the right time, even if the winds of change would test us to see if what we had was meant to last.

At the time, our 40-mile separation seemed like 4,000 miles; so suggests a memory book we began keeping as I headed off for college and she stayed to finish her senior year in high school. Now, on this summer morning nearly three decades later, I sit alone with the book.

Stamps were eight cents when we started writing each other; they featured Dwight "Ike" Eisenhower.

Virtually everyone on my freshman floor had a girlfriend back home—or at another college—and, in a guy sort of way, we proudly talked of how those bonds would never break. A month later, I'm not sure some of those guys could even remember the name of that girl back home.

Me? I couldn't forget about Sally Youngberg. I couldn't forget the way we could talk about life for hours on end. Or how, after a bottle of pop, she felt so comfortable around me she would burp. Or how I came to realize I was a better person for having her in my life.

Once, she sent me this poem:

I love you not only for what you are
but for what I am when I am with you
I love you not only for what you have made of yourself
but for what you are making of me...

I think of who I've become in the last quarter-century—for better or worse. And I think of how Sally has played a part in that—the "better" part. She's softened my edges, slowed me down, dared me to dream.

I lean toward the spontaneous, compulsive, driven side of life. She leans toward the predictable, practical, measured side of life.

She completes me. Without her, I'm a kite with no tail, gyrating in the wind and slamming into some kite-eating tree.

She challenges me: After I'd been in a five-year writing drought, it was Sally who suggested I write a book about fathers and sons. I balked; since an initial book in the early '90s hadn't done as well as I'd expected, I'd been afraid to get back on that literary horse and ride. But this is a subject you know, she insisted. Your father has just died. Your oldest is leaving for college. Write the book, dummy. And I did.

She makes more of me than I could make of myself. When I first met her, I had made a personal commitment to Christ less than two years before. She helped me grow in my faith.

She rides out the storms with me. "Come quickly," said the hospital chaplain. "Your mother is dying."

After three years of commuting, after hundreds of letters, after more Sunday-night goodbyes than I care to remember, we got married. A guitar-playing friend of mine played a song whose words I'd written: "Not Without You," about how tonight I was leaving once again, but not without Sally.

The minister encouraged us to build our life on faith—and live for the stuff beyond ourselves: God and others.

Now, 25 years later, I can still smell the Heaven Scent perfume that somehow got doused on the Memory Book. On one page she wrote:

> *I can't wait until I'm about 50 or so and I reread all of your letters. That is going to be so much fun. Maybe you will be around to read them with me.*

Fifty! My goodness, she wrote of it as if we would be white-haired geezers sitting in our rocking chairs, comparing each other's pill schedules. And yet here we are, about 50—well, 46 and 45—and I'm reading some of these letters and thinking of all that followed that August night we vowed to love each other come what may:

College graduation and U-Hauls and new jobs and first apartments and being on the bottom floor of the duplex with the paper-thin ceiling, hearing the neighbor's cats walk across the kitchen floor.

The day we moved into our first house—it snowed so hard the only way we could get a dresser from truck to house was by putting it into an eight-foot dinghy and sledding it.

The night Ryan was born—afterward, I stood in the hospital parking lot in the middle of the night and looked at the vague outline of the Cascade Mountains and had the magical sense that the world had come to a standstill except for me and Sally and that little baby with the scrunched-up face who was the most beautiful thing I had ever seen.

The night Jason was born—racing through the snow to the hospital in a borrowed VW Bug, our car having been hospitalized for major surgery.

Where does the time go?

The autumn day the car needed fixing and the money simply wasn't there—how we did the only thing we could do, pray, and later that afternoon, Mr. Mac, our retired next-door neighbor, asked if I planned on splitting his wood again that winter.

"Sure," I said. Good, he said, because he'd just received an unexpected insurance dividend and he thought he'd prepay me half of what he was going to pay me—just enough, it turned out, to cover the car.

The excitement and fear of moving to a new city. The worry of going to a children's hospital to see if tiny Jason, our youngest, would grow to be a normal-sized kid. (He would.) The joy of seeing a child's first home run. The pain of Ryan going through hernia surgery, chicken pox, and being fitted for an orthodontic face mask for a profound overbite—all in the same two weeks. The celebration of ten years of marriage. The loneliness of living far away from our extended family for the first time.

The thrill of a phone call saying I'd gotten a job back in Oregon's Willamette Valley, where our roots grow deep. The gut-wrenching agony of gathering two little boys to tell them their cousin Paul was dead, having slipped into an icy river on the last day of 1994. The surprise of calling home one day and getting someone whose deep voice I, at first, didn't recognize, then realized it was Ryan.

Games. Graduations. Growing pains. Sally and I walking on the beach, talking of teenage children and change—how hard it is for the four of us to get our varied expectations to line up for a simple weekend away.

Baseball stadiums. Emergency rooms. Churches—singing "Be Thou My Vision" and looking around to see how blessed we have been with friends who have stood beside us and our children for all these years. New friends coming into our lives. Old friends leaving for new places. Jason not only growing to "normal" size, but making all-league in baseball. Ryan winning two college-conference golf championships.

High-mountain lakes. A kitchen nook that Sally and I built ourselves. Another church setting, only this one a memorial service for my father—how when they played the New Christy

Minstrels' song "Today," Sally gently reached down, took my hand, and put it on top of my mother's.

All of this life and death and disappointment and love shared by two sailors who began in the middle of a lake, huddled beneath a blanket. Now, in the quiet of this summer morning, I can't help but think a simple thought:

God shed His grace on me.

On the Wings of Grace

FIFTEEN MINUTES AFTER TAKEOFF and about 5,000 feet in the air, Tom Boubel turned his Comanche southwest from Spokane, Washington, tucked in the far northeast corner of the state, toward Oregon's Willamette Valley about 330 miles away.

His mood mirrored the sunny skies that his single-engine plane was flying. It was about 5 P.M. on September 16, 1999. A doctor, he had a pressure-filled week of work behind him and a weekend golf tournament with three friends ahead of him.

For the past 23 years, the foursome had gathered once a year to drive, chip, putt, and remember the glory and gags of tournaments past. The four had been friends since high school. They'd played this yearly tournament in sweltering Willamette Valley heat, in driving rain, in high-Cascade Mountains cold. They'd started out as four single guys. Watched one another get married. Watched one another become fathers.

Now, one member of the group—the worst golfer of the four—already had a son about to graduate from college.

That would be me.

I'd known Tom Boubel since we were peppering the blackboards in Miss Weir's sixth-grade class at Jefferson School with spitwads; we had birthdays a month apart. Just a few months before this evening, he'd wished me a happy forty-sixth, and I'd returned the favor a few weeks later.

In junior high, I passed Mr. Chrisman's math class only because Tom Boubel helped me with my homework each morning en route to school on Bus 106. In high school, we trained for cross-country together on summer nights until he

219

somehow blew out a lung while playing his trumpet. After high school, we played in the same Turkey Bowl football game together each Thanksgiving.

Tom was a groomsman at my wedding and I was a groomsman at his. He married a wonderful woman—a nursing student he'd met in medical school—and became a father to two little girls who, like him, have red hair.

In fact, he'd been thinking about that wonderful woman and the two little girls with red hair shortly before he glanced at the RPM gauge on his Comanche's console, a gauge that, in his 11 years of flying that plane, had never been anything but rock steady.

Now, oddly, the gauge oscillated slightly. He tapped it, thinking it was perhaps just sticky. No change.

When you're 5,000 feet in the air, caution rules the day. Boubel contacted Spokane Departure Control and reported a possible mechanical problem. He was returning to the airport, he said, but not declaring an official "emergency."

Then it happened, about halfway through his 180-degree turn: The engine exploded in a blast of sound and smoke. Later, an examination of the aircraft would show that the explosion had ripped an eight-inch hole in the plane's crankcase cover.

The engine and propeller stopped so suddenly that the torque bent the engine mount. A sudden turbulence shook the plane. The prop froze. Grayish-black smoke poured out of the engine. Boubel smelled burning oil.

Amid the sudden chaos, he remembers thinking one simple thought:

I'm going to die.

Though difficult, it is quite possible, after all, to glide an engine-out plane to a successful forced landing; but with the plane also on fire, it is nearly impossible.

Boubel called the tower and declared a full emergency, his voice—based on flight tapes—about two octaves higher than his previous radio transmission. He shut off the fuel to the engine, hoping to stop the fire. Moments later, he discovered the first good news since the chaos had erupted: He was actually *not* on fire.

But almost worse, oil was spraying onto the windshield. (Small planes like this don't come with windshield wipers.) It was like passing a freeway 18-wheeler on one of Oregon's drizzly December days. And at this point, seeing was everything. It was clear he wasn't going to have enough glide time to make it back to Spokane International or even to the rural landing strip the tower had given him coordinates for.

His only chance of survival was finding a highway or farmer's field. Descending at about a thousand feet per minute, he had less than five minutes to make his choice, or the choice would be made for him. In five minutes, the plane would—one way or the other, in some shape or form—be on the ground.

Boubel felt a fear he'd never felt before. Airplanes are built to be light, not to be crash-resistant—or, for that matter, fire-resistant should their fuel tanks rupture. A few years before, a pilot Boubel had known—a pilot he considered more skillful than he was—lost an engine between Spokane and Boise, Idaho, on a nice summer day in a plane much like his. The man did everything right, but the field he chose was too rough, and about 50 feet after touching down, the plane flipped over. He died.

Boubel glanced at his instrument panel, where a sticker said "Glide Speed 105 MPH" and set the plane at that speed. At slower than 75 MPH, the Comanche would stall and corkscrew to earth at 2,000 to 5,000 feet per minute. The area below was a mixture of fields and pine trees.

Through a scant clear spot on the pilot-side of the windshield, he spotted a wheat field that had been laid fallow after the summer crop season. This, he decided, would be it. There was neither time nor altitude for a flyby to see whether the field was smooth enough or unhindered by power lines, ditches, fences, irrigation pipe, and the like.

One chance.

At best, he figured, he would get busted up pretty bad. At worst—well, no time to think about that. No time to say goodbye to Vicky and the girls, and all the others he loved so much, he remembers thinking.

Fly the plane, he thought. *Just fly the plane.*

About a minute before touchdown, he dropped his wheels, remembering what he'd been taught: In a field, the landing gear would probably be torn off but, in the process, would absorb some of the impact.

Boubel had been communicating with the tower ever since reporting the emergency. But now, back at Spokane International, messages elicited no response from the Comanche.

One hundred feet…fifty feet…twenty-five feet…

Then, at a speed nearly 50 MPH faster than most freeway limits, the wheels hit grass. The plane bounced, crabbed right and left, bounced some more. It veered hard toward a grove of large pines. Ahead, Boubel spotted a barbed-wire fence, which could either flip the plane or stop it immediately, much as a cement wall would. He squeezed on the brakes.

Suddenly, all was still.

☾   ☾   ☾

THE ORGANIST AT SPOKANE FIRST PRESBYTERIAN Church opened the service. Soon thereafter, a man walked to the podium to speak.

It was Tom Boubel.

"I am grateful to be alive and have the chance to share with you this morning," he began. "I am also grateful to and humbled by the many people in my church family who've shown their love and their gratitude for my safety.

"Intellectually, I've been aware of how to act and speak as a Christian, but this experience helped me travel the distance from my head to my heart when I speak of gratitude."

By this point, many in the congregation had heard the story or seen it on the eleven-o'clock news a few weeks earlier: how Boubel's plane had landed, stayed intact, and stopped about 25 feet from that fence. Boubel didn't have a scratch on him. He'd walked 45 minutes to a farmer's house and called home.

"Non-Christian friends don't understand when I tell them I was saved by God's amazing grace," Boubel continued. "They credit my landing to skill and luck. But ask any pilot and he will surely tell you: In an engine-out emergency, if you get the plane to the ground, what happens on the ground is still out of your hands—in my case, it was in God's hands."

Certainly, his being an anesthesiologist, and having faced half a dozen situations in which a patient's life had hung in the balance, had taught Boubel to stay calm in emergencies. But why, he wondered, were the winds so calm? Often, evening winds near Spokane blew strong, which would have severely complicated the landing.

Why, six days before the accident, had he somehow felt compelled to make a "Glide Speed 105 MPH" label and stick it to the instrument panel? The only time you need such information is when you've lost your engine, which hadn't happened to him in 25 years of flying.

And what about a smooth field being in the right place at the right time? "God put the right field in front of me," Boubel told a TV reporter.

Now, standing in front of his congregation, he explained how the accident had changed him.

"As a Christian," he said, "I don't believe in fate or luck. God loves us too much to leave our lives up to chance. In my mind and in my heart, I know now that every blessing of my life, no matter how small, is a gift from God. Each moment of every day has a blessing from God if you look at it with a heart of gratitude."

The accident, he later told me, taught him that God isn't through with him yet. That "the Christian life is about relationships with other people—not just loved ones, but everyone we meet in our journey."

He learned how many people cared about him.

He learned how precious life is.

He learned how much time we spend worrying about the trivialities of life. "The most obvious change in me is how difficult it is for me to seriously complain about anything now," he said. "I have always been an in-control type person, and a fairly perfectionist type to boot. That nature makes me fairly critical of myself and situations around me. But now it's hard for me to spend much time and energy complaining—or listening to others complain—because God's spirit stirs my memory about the crash. Money and possessions are just *stuff,* and God cares about *us,* not our *stuff.*"

The Centerpiece

IT WAS THE CHRISTMAS WHEN I HEARD all the carols but never listened to the words, the Christmas when I was more burdened with questions than buoyed with answers. I was in college and life had gotten blurry.

Like everyone else, I had spent the past few weeks going through the motions, the holiday equivalent of toothbrushing. Not something you did because you were compelled to do so, but because it was part of life's routines.

I had done the expected: bought presents, sang songs. I looked at the residential light displays, including the manger scene with the shepherds gathered around the Christ child while Santa watched approvingly from the roof of the manger.

Now it was Christmas Day, the cymbal clash at the end of the drum roll.

But where was the magic?

Certainly not in the weather. Like most Christmases in Oregon, it was one of those in-between days—too cold to be pleasant, too warm to snow. It was one of those drab days when you wanted the weather to do something—suddenly muster itself into a driving rainstorm or break into soul-cleansing sunshine. *Anything.* But it would not.

As we made our way north to my uncle's home in Oregon's Willamette Valley, the clouds hung low over the Coast Range and, like my own overcast mood, showed no signs of clearing. White Christmases, I had decided, were reserved for schmaltzy movies and television commercials in which everybody was so busy smiling and hugging and spreading holiday cheer that they didn't stop to consider what the celebration was all about.

Two thousand years ago, a bunch of ragged shepherds had seen a star in the sky—a message of the Messiah, of healing, of hope. As we drove along, it all seemed so far away; not 2,000 years away, but light-years away. I looked at the houses as we drove by, imagining families eating dinner and opening presents and watching football on TV.

But where was the message?

Certainly not in our modern-day celebrations. On this day, the sign in the sky was not a star, but the smokestack of a paper plant. We always drove by the paper plant en route to my uncle's house, and Christmas Day was the lone day of the year when it didn't operate. That was our sign, our reminder that a child has been born. *Rejoice! For unto freeway passengers in the State of Oregon is given a day which is stench-free.*

We arrived at my uncle's house, four more people in a diverse mix linked not by common interests or values, but by blood. There had been a time when I had keenly felt part of this clan, as if returning each year had been like putting on a pair of well-worn tennis shoes that fit just right.

This year, I felt no such comfort. Perhaps it was my age. In my late teens, I was too old to believe in the magic of Santa Claus, too young to believe in children's laughter, too collegiate to be engrossed in the Christmas story, too confused to be anything other than a cynic in holiday disguise.

This was my year of questioning, the year I wanted to quit college, stop writing, and become a milkman; the year my faith had been battered by so many self-righteous professors and self-indulgent dorm neighbors that I had almost come to believe it was easier to switch than fight.

Where was the meaning?

Certainly not in this living room of people, I thought as I half-listened to the small talk. They were good folks, but it was all so programmed: the same people. The same house. The same conversations. The same guitar-only Christmas music playing softly on the stereo.

It was all warm and comfortable and cozy—we seemingly had it all—and yet it left me empty, as if something were missing. We ate the same kind of food we ate every year. We made all the same too-full jokes about how much we'd overeaten. We made the same small talk.

Then it happened. As we prepared to open our presents—the last stop on this train ride of tradition—my uncle stood up in front of us and said he had something he wanted to share with us. People looked puzzled. This was not part of the routine. This was not written in the script.

My uncle looked around the room. He said he had been thinking and had decided it was important to remember why we celebrated Christmas. He wanted to read something to help remind us.

I figured he would read us the Christmas story—that's a safe choice at Christmas—but he did not. Instead, he read us a piece written a long time ago, a piece called "One Solitary Life":

> *Here is a man who was born of Jewish parents,*
> *The child of a peasant woman...*
> *He never wrote a book.*
> *He never held an office.*
> *He never owned a home.*
> *He never had a family.*
> *He never went to college.*
> *He never put foot inside a big city.*
> *He never traveled two hundred miles from the place*
> *   where he was born.*
> *He never did one of the things that usually accom-*
> *   pany greatness.*
> *He had no credentials but himself...*

The two dozen people in the living room were still. No one even whispered. We all just looked at my uncle as he continued, realizing that we were in the midst of something strangely special.

> *While He was still a young man,*
> *The tide of popular opinion turned against Him.*
> *His friends ran away.*
> *One of them denied Him...*
> *He was nailed to a cross between two thieves.*
> *His executioners gambled for the only piece of property*
> *   He had on earth...His coat.*
> *When He was dead,*
> *He was taken down and laid in a borrowed grave*
> *   through the pity of a friend.*

My uncle's eyes grew misty. So did some others'. So did mine.

> *Nineteen wide centuries have come and gone,*
> *And He is the centerpiece of the human race*
> *And the leader of the column of progress.*
> *I am far within the mark*
> *When I say that all the armies that ever marched,*
> *And all the navies that were ever built...*
> *Have not affected the life of man upon earth*
> *As powerfully as has that One Solitary Life.*

Had this been the movies, a light snow would have begun to fall outside. But snow did not begin falling. Nor did a star appear in the sky. Instead, my uncle simply sat down. Slowly, people began making small talk again before opening presents.

I don't know how the reading affected others. I only know that for me, it was more than a temporary cease-fire for my inner turmoil. It was light amidst the darkness. It was reassurance that the son of that peasant woman had grown into humankind's hope. It was a reminder that, amidst the routine, what had been missing on this Christmas Day was not snow on the ground or a star in the sky.

What had been missing was the One who'd promised to see us through—in John Newton's words—the many dangers, toils, and snares, the One whose grace had brought us safe thus far and whose grace would lead us home.

What had been missing—both on this day and in my life— had been the guest of honor, the centerpiece of the celebration.

Looking Back

ALL GOOD THINGS MUST END, we're told, even summer. Which is why, one late-August night as I skirted the western shores of Fern Ridge Lake in *At Last,* I found myself slipping into one of those reflective moods. It would be my last sail of the summer; soon, autumn would come and the water would go—drained to the sea so Oregon's infamous winter rains could fill the reservoir instead of flooding the valley as they used to each year.

You can smell and feel and see the end of summer. Here in Oregon, out on a lake, you smell a waft of smoke from the grass-seed fields that have been burned after harvest. You feel just the slightest tinge of coolness in the evening air, a tinge you wouldn't feel in June or July. You see the occasional empty slip in the moorage and realize another boat is gone, a victim of the natural order of the seasons and the winter that inevitably must come.

Tiller in hand, a light breeze in my face, I looked back and, even at five knots, the wake of the boat was pronounced, spreading evenly behind me like a flight of geese in their "V" formation. A boat plies the waters and leaves a wake, as do we when plying life's waters.

I think of a friend of mine, Matt, and his father, who was in the final stages of cancer. One October night I drove an hour to see the man, who was at home, sitting in a wheelchair, hooked to an oxygen tank. He was weak and tired, but his handshake was firm and he made me feel welcome. His sentences came slowly and deliberately, like the brushstrokes of an artist who knows what the final picture needs to look like but who chooses to paint a little, step back, consider what he's painted, then paint some more.

We talked for a little more than an hour. Then he grew tired and needed to sleep. I shook his hand once again and was gone, driving into the night, thinking about fathers and sons; thinking about my own father, now gone more than four years; thinking about life and death and the wakes we leave.

The next morning, when I arrived at work, I found a recorded message on my phone answering machine. It was from Matt, choking back tears as he spoke. Thanks for coming to see my dad, he said. He just died.

In the time since, I've thought a lot about that one-hour slice of time I spent with the man—his last night on earth. About what seemed to matter to him.

When Matt had left to fetch a couple of pops, I had told the man that he'd raised a good son, a son he could be proud of. And I watched as the man's eyes grew misty. Later, as we talked about a book I'd written about the connection between fathers and sons—*A Father for All Seasons*—he grew even more emotional.

He and the others in the room—Matt, Matt's mother, and Matt's uncle—started talking about the memories. They talked of growing up in Indiana, Matt's mom and dad meeting, family vacations, places they had lived, children and grandchildren—stuff that, at the time, had probably seemed like the routine rhythm of life but now, in the end, read like epic poetry, even if it was only a story about Matt getting in trouble for some Dennis-the-Menace prank.

When we're on our deathbeds, I was reminded, this is the kind of stuff that will matter. Not the headlines, but the memories that maybe only a handful of people even know about. Not world history, but family history. Not what you've accomplished for the masses, but what you've experienced with your family.

And, I was reminded, the common denominator is this: relationships.

It's been said that nobody, while on his deathbed, ever wished he'd spent more time at the office. Likewise, I doubt that many people on their deathbeds ponder their net worth or feel smug about having had a better car than the Joneses next door or consider themselves successes because they accomplished every task on their Palm Pilot.

"I have seen all the things that are done under the sun," wrote the author of Ecclesiastes. "All of them are meaningless, a chasing after the wind" (1:14).

I believe people reflect on just a handful of things while on their deathbeds: not only what is to come, but on what *was* and what could have been in relation to those around them. Relational victories and defeats. Reconciliation and regret. But not on dying with the most toys, having the largest portfolio, or finishing highest on the bestsellers list.

"And I saw that all labor and all achievement spring from man's envy of his neighbor. This too is meaningless, a chasing after the wind" (Ecclesiastes 4:4).

At Matt's father's memorial service, another of the man's three sons, Mike, sang a rendition of a song I've long liked, though I've never heard it sung so much from the heart. It was an old Dan Fogelberg song called "Leader of the Band," sung from a son to his aging father.

It's about a "quiet man of music" who passes on his love of songs to a son. Toward the end, a line says, "And, papa, I don't think I said 'I love you' near enough…" When Mike got to that line, he opened his mouth to sing but, choked with emotion, could only whisper the words. And yet what he whispered spoke volumes about what matters in the end: People. Love. And our expression of that love to them.

When it's our last night on earth, what will matter to us? When it's our memorial service, what will those left behind say of us? When it's our slip in the moorage that is suddenly empty, how will we have spent our life: chasing after the fickle winds of materialism or allowing the winds of grace to fill our sails?

> *As for a man, his days are like grass,*
> *he flourishes like a flower of the field;*
> *the wind blows over it and it is gone,*
> *and its place remembers it no more.*

—*Psalm 103:15-16*

On that last sail of summer, I headed *At Last* south toward a place I've come to call Grace Cove, where the waters are usually calm, and found myself thinking of my father, the man who taught me to sail. I remembered a letter he once wrote, a rarity for a man who seldom put pen to paper. A portion of the two-page letter said this:

> *As I told you on the phone, Bob, we won't be leaving you much cash, only a house, and I want you to consider this your boat. Sure, Mom and I will have some great times on her, but someday she will be yours. We will take the greatest care of her and I can't imagine any of us ever wanting anything bigger or better.*

Nor can I. It is a privilege to sail this boat, an act of grace. Yes, I will take great care of her. And no, I can't imagine wanting anything bigger or better either. l like this boat, simple and small though she may be.

She is filled with memories of my mother and father at their life-loving best; of that early date Sally and I had, becalmed in a rainstorm and loving every second of it; of two little boys asleep in the cabin and me lying outside in my sleeping bag, looking at the stars and feeling small and insignificant and yet, having been made by the One who made those stars, feeling also strangely, wonderfully significant.

Ready about, I said to myself, and thrust the tiller to the port side. The boat came about, the boom flopped from one side to the other, and an evening breeze billowed my sails anew. Ahead, the cove welcomed me home. Behind, the boat's wake rolled toward distant shores.

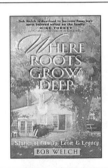
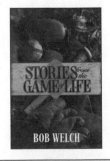